T0171458

GOD'S LOVE FOR US

OUR CHRISTIAN FOUNDATION

GOD'S LOVE FOR US

OUR CHRISTIAN FOUNDATION

JEAN ANNE STUBBLEFIELD

WESTBOW
PRESS
A DIVISION OF THOMAS NELSON

Copyright © 2013 Jean Anne Stubblefield.

All rights reserved. No part of this book may be used or reproduced by any means, graphic, electronic, or mechanical, including photocopying, recording, taping or by any information storage retrieval system without the written permission of the publisher except in the case of brief quotations embodied in critical articles and reviews.

WestBow Press books may be ordered through booksellers or by contacting:

WestBow Press
A Division of Thomas Nelson
1663 Liberty Drive
Bloomington, IN 47403
www.westbowpress.com
1-(866) 928-1240

Because of the dynamic nature of the Internet, any web addresses or links contained in this book may have changed since publication and may no longer be valid. The views expressed in this work are solely those of the author and do not necessarily reflect the views of the publisher, and the publisher hereby disclaims any responsibility for them.

Unless otherwise indicated, all Scripture quotations are taken from the New International Version of the Holy Bible, NEW INTERNATIONAL VERSION. Copyright © 1973, 1978, 1984 Biblica. Used by permission of Zondervan. All rights reserved.

Scripture quotations marked KJV are from the King James Version of the Bible.

Scripture quotations marked NKJV are taken from the New King James Version. Copyright © 1979, 1980, 1982 by Thomas Nelson, Inc. Used by permission. All rights reserved.

Scripture quotations marked (AMP) are from the Amplified Bible, Copyright © 1954, 1958, 1962, 1964, 1965, 1987 by the Lockman Foundation. Used by permission.

ISBN: 978-1-4497-7932-0 (sc)
ISBN: 978-1-4497-7933-7 (e)

Library of Congress Control Number: 2012923505

Printed in the United States of America
WestBow Press rev. date: 1/7/2013

It is my joy to dedicate this book to Craig—my husband, best friend and confidant, brother in Christ and now my Pastor. We have been on this journey into Love together since the Lord joined us 18 years ago. Craig has been a spiritual rock through all our travels and all our ups and downs in following the Lord's plan for our lives. He has become a wealth of revelation as we have given ourselves to the study of God's grace and love for us which is the Gospel of the Lord Jesus Christ. Many of the truths contained in this writing have been spoken from his lips during the anointed teaching and preaching of our church services. Thank you, Craig, for all you've been to me. I am a better person because of you, and I look forward to many more years of exploring the depths of our Father's love together with you—even throughout eternity in His Presence!

TABLE OF CONTENTS

Introduction 1

1. God Is Love 9

2. Jesus—God's Love Revealed 25

3. God's Love—Our Christian Foundation 43

4. You Are God's Beloved In Christ 65

5. Living A Life Of Love 85

INTRODUCTION

Love lifted me.
Love lifted me.
When nothing else could help,
Love lifted me.

Lying in the cool, dark upstairs bedroom of the old farmhouse, I turned and faced the wall. My life had been careening out of control in a crazy downward spiral until I now found myself at the bottom of a horrible pit. My mother's words spoken to me earlier, as we sat in our country kitchen, still rang in my ears, "Jeanie, you just need Jesus." Hadn't I been there and done that? Wasn't I raised as a Christian, attending church every Sunday and Wednesday? Wasn't I a recipient of the Queen with Scepter award in GA's, and didn't I possess a stack of Vacation Bible School Certificates? Hadn't I made my profession of faith and been baptized? Yes, I'd been there. I'd done that. And yet my heart was breaking with years of disappointments, abuses and condemnation. I had even spent years exploring and implementing Eastern religious practices into my New Age concept of life. I had decided to believe in Reincarnation, and I was a strict adherent to the Macrobiotic way of eating and its accompanying philosophy. I had explored and tried to leave no stone unturned in my search to reach God, or as I called Him, the Universal Power. Now, at thirty-one years of age I lay broken, hurting and confused in this dark bedroom, facing the wall. "Jesus, if You are God's Son, and if You really do love me, I need You to show me," I prayed the first prayer I'd prayed in unremembered years. It was the most serious and desperate plea I had ever made in my life.

Several weeks later, I sat cross-legged on the soft green grass in my backyard. It was an unusually warm and sunny day in March. I was practicing Transcendental Meditation in which I had been professionally trained. My fingers were in position, hands resting on my knees, and I was repeating my mantra over and over. By practicing TM, I was trying to sink down into the only kind of peace I had known in recent years. Suddenly, as I sat there chanting my mantra (which I later found out was the name of a Hindu god), I saw in a vision Jesus; He was walking towards me, and in so doing proving that He truly is God—preempting any other so-called god that one could call upon. He was smiling at me beautifully. More than noticing His features, I was overwhelmed with His love that flowed over me in waves. Love that flowed from His heart and through His eyes to me! My first words were, "Oh my God, You are really real!", for before this moment, I did not truly know that Jesus was alive and real. He was always something of a fictional character to me. From that moment I was forever His! I was forever changed—changed by love! My life made a 180 degree turn, and I began walking a new path with Jesus. His love had lifted me out of my horrible pit, set my feet upon a rock and given me a brand new life!

But that is not the end of a beautiful story where I lived happily ever after. And it is "the rest of the story" that compels me to write this book. For what happened to me in "the rest of the story" is what happens to multitudes of Christians following the glorious freedom of the Father's love given to them in the New Birth. I was baptized in the Holy Spirit two months following my New Birth in Christ. I began attending a Bible believing, Bible teaching, Spirit filled church. At this point, the Bible became very real to me, and I began devouring it with zeal. But something sinister was happening to me without me even realizing it, which is exactly what the enemy of my soul, the devil, wanted to achieve in my life. I was taught what was termed "practical righteousness" which, although an erroneous teaching, is the well-meaning and accepted concept for most modern Christians as well as Christian leaders and teachers. I was taught that, yes, I was saved absolutely by grace through faith in Jesus and not of works lest any man should boast; but now that I was saved, I was taught that I must maintain my right standing and fellowship with God through my works. Because of this I stepped into the world of "trying"— trying to please God, trying to serve Him and prove my love for Him. Oh, I loved Him so much and wanted Him to know it! Like most other serious Christians I knew, I began living a life in God that, in my mind, was based on how much I loved God and proving my love for Him by how much I did for God. In other words, I entered onto the performance treadmill of Christianity. I believed that my rightness with God—my close fellowship with Him—was based upon my performance. How very wrong this path proved to be. This teaching is not based on the New Testament (New Covenant) teachings, but on a mixture of the Old and New Covenants and a lot of religious traditions. In following this teaching, I became self-righteous without even being aware of it, depending more upon my works unto God than on His finished work on the cross for me. I had fallen into a snare that crippled me and kept me from living the life of freedom that Christ died to give me. I did not realize the simple truth that the only way to be close to the Father is to completely trust in Jesus and everything He had already accomplished for me on the cross, and to live my life out of my love relationship with Christ alone.

I was, during this time of my Christian life, definitely full of passion, zeal and lots of good works, even to the point of burn-out; but somehow, no matter how hard I tried, I never felt totally accepted or as though I completely measured up. I did not believe that I was totally qualified to receive all that God had promised in His Word. I always felt that there was something I wasn't doing quite right that was keeping me back, and (God forbid) I even, at times, felt like God was my problem and not my solution!

I lived this way for twenty-four years. To be sure, the life I received after simply accepting Christ and His love into my heart was far superior to anything I had previously experienced in my life, and I had wonderful times with the Lord and learned many beautiful truths. My worst day as a Christian far exceeded my life without Christ! But during those twenty-four years, I never truly experienced the freedom, victory, peace, joy and rest that is promised in the New Testament and is available to all Believers every minute of every day. I was "trying" to do everything right, but to a large degree was not experiencing what God had promised me in His Word. I had begun my walk with the Lord based on the realization that He was alive and that He loved me with His whole heart, but I then mistakenly let go of His gracious love given in Christ and began trying to keep self-imposed and man-imposed requirements in order to please God. The terrible part of this experience was that, to me, this was the "standard" of Christianity because most serious Christians I knew lived this same way in their walk with the Lord. Admitting that it wasn't working for me was not an option since we all knew, "There's nothing wrong with God, and there's nothing wrong with His Word." Therefore the problem had to be with me; and this I already knew, but I did not know how to fix me.

My husband and I were called to the ministry, and the Lord led us to relocate in order to attend ministry school in Florida. We left house, land, business, mothers, children, brothers and sisters—all—to follow the Lord. We also visited other nations and did mission work during this time. In total, we lived in Florida for five years in the red-hot atmosphere of the Brownsville Revival, and we then relocated again following the Lord's leading. We spent three and a half years in Fort Worth, TX working, ministering and learning. After those three and a half years, we were directed to move back to our hometown to begin our own ministry. We were sent out and licensed through Kenneth Copeland Ministries, the ministry we were affiliated with in Fort Worth. I tell you this so that you can see we were not what would be classified as "nominal Christians" or the "nod to God crowd". We were seriously seeking God and His plan for our lives, laying down all to find it, and yet we were not completely satisfied with our experience as Christians because our Christian foundation was built on a few wrong beliefs from the beginning of our walk with Christ. We were seeing the Word of God through our own "filter" which was not completely based on truth. The enemy, the devil, was using this to keep us from experiencing our total freedom and victory in Christ. It is because of these issues that I feel compelled to write this book. I desire to share the revelation that has totally transformed our lives and has caused us to experience the deep, abiding satisfaction, peace and blessedness of the eternal life that Jesus died to make available to us. And it is available to all who call on the Name of Jesus in faith. It is available to you! I pray that as you read the words of this book, the Holy Spirit will kindle a desire in your heart to know these truths, and that in knowing these truths and continuing to live in them, you will be made free indeed!

GOD IS LOVE 1

God is love. What a seemingly simple statement, but in those three little words lie the entire Gospel message and even the very essence of all creation! Many of us have heard these words, "God is love", or the words, "For God so loved the world…" so often and for so many years that we have begun to only give them a quick, mental nod without seriously considering the life-giving truth of these statements. We as Christians tend to quickly say, "Yes, I already know that God loves me," as if this were the kindergarten of Christianity and then move on to the so-called *deeper things* in the Word of God. We don't really understand that it is by the knowledge of God's love for us individually that we live in union with Him and flow effortlessly in faith, grace, peace and joy as Christians. And because we think we already *know* that God loves us, we do not take the time or expend the energy needed to really delve into the depths of God by knowing Him as a good God who always does good and loves us because He is love itself. He is the source of love from which all true love flows. Love originated with God. Love is who He is. His every motive, desire and thought is born out of His love and desire to do us only good always. It is impossible for God to do, say or think evil. It is impossible for God to lie or cheat. It is impossible for God to kill, steal or destroy (*See John 10:10*). Since He is the creator of all things and also the One who sustains all things and holds them together, if He did evil, the whole universe would crumble and fall apart. All creation exists out of the integrity and honesty of God's Word which reveals Him as love.

Whoever does not love does not know God, because God is love.
1John 4:8

...God is love. Whoever lives in love lives in God, and God in him. *1John 4:16*

In order to better understand the traits or characteristics of love (God), we must allow the Bible to interpret the Bible. In *1Corinthians 13:4-8, 13* we find Paul giving a detailed description of love by the inspiration of God's Holy Spirit.

Love is patient, love is kind. It does not envy, it does

not boast, it is not proud. It is not rude, it is not self-seeking, it is not easily angered, it keeps no record of wrongs. Love does not delight in evil but rejoices with the truth. It always protects, always trusts, always hopes, always perseveres. Love never fails. (13) And now these three remain: faith, hope and love. But the greatest of these is love.

This scripture is God's definition of His kind of love. It is who God is and how He operates. In order to see this more clearly, we can remove the word *love* and replace it with *God* for the purposes of our study. We can do this for study purposes because God is love (*1John 4:8 &16*), or, we can say, God equals love. Since God=love, then love=God. The two words are interchangeable. Let's read the same scripture exchanging the word *love* with the word *God* to receive a greater revelation of God.

God is patient, God is kind. God does not envy, God does not boast, God is not proud. God is not rude, God is not self-seeking, God is not easily angered, God keeps no record of wrongs. God does not delight in evil, but rejoices with the truth. God always protects, God always trusts, God always hopes, God always perseveres. Now these three remain, faith, hope and God. But the greatest of these is God.

How does this description of God compare to your understanding of Him? If you are like most of us, your personal picture of God has not been painted quite so beautifully or graciously. Why do we so often see God in such an unlovely, negative and distorted way? The reason for this is that there is a devil loose in the earth whose sole task is to paint a picture of God in our hearts that is contrary to what God says about Himself in His Word. It is sad to say that even God's own people often have a distorted and perverse view of Him. Why does the devil want to lie and deceive us about our wonderful God of love? It is because he knows that if we get discouraged enough because of erroneous thinking—thinking that convinces us that God is our problem—we will not be able to receive our bountiful inheritance in Christ. He knows that through discouragement many may even depart the faith or at best become ineffective and fearful Christians. Beloved, *fearful* should never be an adjective used to describe a Christian, for fear is the opposite of love!

Yes, in this passage of scripture Paul is laying out the standard of God's kind of love which is called *agape* love. He is telling us how we, as Christians, should relate to others; but first and foremost, we must know that this standard is who God is and how He relates to us.

Without building our entire Christian foundation on knowing and receiving a greater revelation of God's love for us, we will never have the ability to truly love others with His kind of agape love. As we begin to know God as Love and allow Him to fill our hearts with Himself, His love will overflow out of our hearts to others. He does not expect us to "work up" this kind of love to give to others; in fact, we cannot work it up because it is supernatural love and can only be received from God in order to be given out to others. Human love is very natural and limited, but God's love perseveres and never fails. We are simply to know Him, live in Him, be filled with Him and allow His own love flow *to us*. It will then flow *through us* to others as our hearts are tendered by His love.

As we examine the description of God (who is love) in *1Corinthians 13*, let's really think about what is being said.

- **God is patient.** He is not impatient, irritated, edgy, intolerant, exasperated, aggravated, irked or touchy.

- **God is kind.** He is not unkind, mean, ruthless, cruel, wicked, callous, heartless or hurtful in any way.

- **God does not envy anyone**. Everything was created by and belongs to God. He has no need to envy anyone their possessions or position.

- **God is not boastful (but humble).** Jesus is our example. He was God in the flesh. … Who (Jesus) being in very nature God, did not consider equality with God something to be grasped, but made Himself nothing, taking the very nature of a servant, being made in human likeness… *Philippians 2:6-7*

- **God is not proud or haughty.** God's Son, Jesus, wrapped a towel around Himself and washed the feet of the disciples. *(See John 13:3-5, 13-16)*

- **God is never rude**. He is not ill-mannered, impolite, discourteous, disrespectful, uncouth, foul, or vulgar.

- **God is not self-seeking.** He is not self-centered, but cares about others. He chose to give His only beloved Son to become a human being, suffer and be murdered in order to take away our sin and our curse rather than to keep Him for Himself and allow humanity to be cursed and destined to Hell. *(See John 3:16)* He placed our well-being above His own.

- **God does not become angry easily.** God is slow to anger. The Lord is compassionate and gracious slow to anger, abounding in love.
  Psalm 103:8

- **God keeps no record of wrongs.** For as high as the heavens are above the earth, so great is His love for those who fear Him; **as far as the east is from the west, so far has He removed our transgressions from us**. *Psalm 103:11-12*

  For I will forgive their wickedness and **will remember their sins no more**. *Jeremiah 31:34b*

- **God never delights in evil happenings.** (Jesus said,) The thief (the devil) comes not but to steal, kill and destroy, but I (Jesus) have come that they might have life and have it to the full. *John 10:10*. God's will is for us to have a wonderful, blessed, joyful, abundant life.

- **God always protects His own.** Read *Psalm 91*. Jesus is the *secret place,* and in Him we rest under God's shadow. This entire Psalm tells us of

God's great protection over us when we are in Christ through our faith in Him.

- **God always trusts us—His children.** When we are born again through faith in Christ Jesus, we are sealed by the indwelling Holy Spirit. This is God's very own Spirit **in us.** God trusts us because He has given us Himself to be in us to counsel, guide and direct us.

- **God always hopes the best for us.** In Christ He has given us everything we need for life and Godliness. *(See 2Peter1:3).* His desire is that we acquire revelation knowledge and truth through the study of His Word in order to access all that we have been given, and to live the abundant life He came to give us *(See John 10:10).*

- **God always perseveres.** God never, ever gives up on us! He is always working His plan. God never fails! ...for He (God) Himself has said, I will not in any way fail you nor give you up nor leave you without support. I will not, I will not, I will not in any degree leave you-assuredly not! *Hebrews 13:5(AMP)*

- **Of faith, hope and love, the greatest of these**

is love or God! As we set ourselves to know and believe in God's love for us, our faith and hope will flow easily and effectively.

For in Christ Jesus neither circumcision nor uncircumcision avail anything but **faith working through love**. *Galatians 5:6*

Now hope does not disappoint, because the **love of God has been poured out in our hearts by the Holy Spirit**. *Romans 5:5*

Knowing God as He truly is according to His Word, is an ongoing revelation that we will continue to grow in until we reach our Heavenly home, and, I believe we will continue to grow in this revelation even in Heaven. We can see Paul's revelation of knowing God's love in the prayers he prayed for the churches. In *Philippians 1:9* he prayed, "And this is my prayer that **your love may abound more and more in knowledge and depth of insight**, so that you may be able to discern what is best..." As we grow more and more in the correct knowledge of God and in depth of insight into His true nature of love, we will be able to discern what is best for us in our lives. The decisions we make will be right because they will be discerned through the Spirit of God's love in us. As we know and trust in the fact that God loves us unconditionally, we will prosper in life, for this is His desire for us. We will know and

walk in what is best for us as judged by God's love…
and LOVE NEVER FAILS! We will never fail because
God loves us! In *Exodus 34:5* God is revealing Himself
to Moses,

Then the Lord came down in the cloud and stood there with him
and proclaimed His Name, the Lord. And He passed in front of
Moses proclaiming, **The Lord, the Lord, the compassionate
and gracious God, slow to anger, abounding in love and
faithfulness, maintaining love to thousands and forgiving
wickedness, rebellion and sin**.

God is GOOD! God is LOVE! God is FOR us! He is on
our side! From beginning to end throughout all eternity,
God is LOVE and HE LOVES US!

In *Ephesians 3:17,* Paul prays,

…and I pray that you, being rooted and established in love may
have power, together with all the saints, to grasp how wide and
long and high and deep is the love of Christ and to know this love
that surpasses knowledge—that you may be filled to the measure
of all the fullness of God.

What an awesome scripture! Paul is telling us that when
we are established in love, in God, and in the truth of
who God is and how He deeply loves us, we can actually
be filled to the measure of all the fullness of God!
This is an incredible statement. It surpasses our human

understanding and knowledge, but our born-again spirit can grasp this knowledge of God, of His love, and we can be filled with all the fullness of our God! No wonder our enemy, the devil, wants to pull the wool over our eyes and paint an inaccurate and destructive picture of God in our hearts and minds. He will stop at nothing to keep us from knowing the truth about God. When we set our hearts to really know this love, God will stop at nothing to bring us the light of His truth on the subject. God is love, and He chooses to love us!

I would like to relate a parable that Jesus told in order to explain the love of His Father for His people. We find this text in *Luke 15:11-24*. It is the story of a father who had two sons in his house. The youngest son asked the father for his inheritance, and the father gave his inheritance to him. The young man then left his father's house and went to another country. There he squandered all of his inheritance on wild and riotous living. After all of his money was gone, a famine came to that country, and the only job the young man could find was feeding pigs. He was so hungry he wanted to eat the pig food, but no one gave him anything. One day while he was feeding the pigs, he came to his senses. He remembered his father's house and knew that his father's servants had plenty to eat. He decided to go back and tell his father that he was no longer worthy to be called his son and ask him to hire him as one of his servants. The Bible says that,

…while he was still a long way off his father saw him and was filled with compassion for him. He ran to his son, threw his arms around him and kissed him. *Luke 15:20*

Wow! In this story that Jesus told, we see some of God's attributes of love in action.

- *The father was looking for his son.* He was looking far into the distance hoping to see him coming. He obviously had a habit of looking for his son every day, hoping and believing that he would one day see his son returning home. **God always hopes! God always perseveres!**

- *The father was filled with compassion when he saw his son.* **God, our Father, is patient. God is kind. God is not easily angered. God keeps no record of wrongs.**

- *The father ran to his son.* He ran to him and threw his arms around him and kissed him even though he still smelled of pigs and had wasted all his inheritance. The father didn't even know for certain what was on that son's mind. He could have been coming back to demand more money.

The father didn't know that the son's heart was repentant when he was running to meet him. The father had already forgiven his son and wanted to express his love for his son with an embrace. **God keeps no record of wrongs—**

> …and their sins I will remember no more.
>
> *Jeremiah 31:34*

No matter how we have failed and messed things up, we simply need to come back to our Father in order for His love to be poured out on us. Our first response needs to be to run to our Father, God. He is waiting and looking to see us coming, and He will not withhold His love from us but will lavish us with mercy and grace through Jesus Christ.

In the Gospels of the New Testament—Matthew, Mark, Luke and John—we read about the life of Jesus as He ministered and lived His life on earth. We are also told in *Acts 10:38* that He,

> …went about doing good and healing all who were oppressed by the devil.

As the record of His life shows, He did good everywhere He went. John actually tells us in *John 21:25* that,

...there are also many other things that Jesus did, which if they were written one by one I suppose that even the world itself could not contain the books that would be written.

In Jesus' own words recorded in *John 14:9*, He tells us,

> "If you have seen Me, you have seen the Father."

Jesus is making a point to tell us that He is God in the flesh. In other words, if God Almighty, Maker of Heaven and Earth and everything in them, stepped out of eternity and came to earth, He would look just like Jesus, and He would do exactly the same works that Jesus did while on earth. In fact, this is precisely what did happen, for Jesus is the exact representation of God's being according to *Hebrews 1:2*. Jesus came to earth as God in human form. He was fully God and fully man. When we look at the life of Jesus and the things that He did, we see the very heart and nature of God. Jesus went about doing good. Jesus went about loving people, helping people, healing people and doing good to people. Seeing Jesus is seeing God. Hearing Jesus is hearing God. Jesus came to show us that God is love through the life He lived and through the sacrificial death He died.

> Greater love has no one than this, that he lay down his life for his friends. *John 15:13*

Jesus is God in human form. Jesus is Love in human form. He went about doing good because He is Love, and Love always does what is good and right. He came to bless us and give us back our relationship with God through our faith in His death, burial and resurrection. He came to make our lives better, easier and blessed. He came to deliver us from heavy burdens, cares, distress, fear and anxiety. Love always desires to help, to lift others up and to bless them. He did not come representing His Father as a tyrant, lording it over His people with harshness, cruelty or heavy, burdening loads for us to bear. He came in gentleness and humility helping and loving His creation and lifting them up to His level even though it cost Him His very life to do it. God is good! God is Love! Jesus reveals God's loving nature as the God-man in *Matthew 11:28-30(AMP)*.

Come to Me, all you who labor and are heavy-laden and overburdened, and I will cause you to rest [I will ease and relieve and refresh your souls]. Take My yoke upon you and learn of Me, for I am gentle (meek) and humble (lowly) in heart and you will find rest (relief and ease and refreshment and recreation and blessed quiet) for your souls. For My yoke is wholesome (useful, good— not harsh, hard, sharp, or pressing, but comfortable, gracious and pleasant) and My burden is light and easy to be borne.

What an awesome loving God! He is so gracious, so kind! He has given us a Savior, Jesus, who is God and who represented His Father perfectly as Love. God is Love, and Love had to find a way to give His creation a pathway back into fellowship with Him. That Love came to earth as Jesus. Jesus reveals the heart of God to us by telling us that living with God is supposed to be light and easy, restful and refreshing. He instructs us to learn of Him; therefore, let us do just that! Let's learn of Jesus. Let's explore and mine out the treasures of knowing and learning more of God, who is Love, so that we may partake more fully of the rest—relief, ease, refreshment, recreation and blessed quiet—that He has provided for us to live in because of His great and immeasurable love for us!

JESUS—GOD'S LOVE REVEALED

2

For God so loved the world that He gave His only begotten Son that whosoever believes on Him should not perish but have everlasting life. *John 3:16*

How many times we have heard this wonderful portion of scripture! Most of us, as Christians or having been raised in Christian families, cut our spiritual teeth on this verse. But having committed it to memory, have we really meditated and thought on it, seeking a better understanding of the love of God contained in it? I am impressed that the verse does not simply say, "For God loved the world...," but that, "For God **so** loved the world." The Holy Spirit is making a point here. This is not a casual or general blanket kind of love, but an emphatic, focused, intense, heart-consuming love! God, who is love, **so loved** the world! God in His infinite wisdom and understanding and knowledge of each person on the earth, throughout all time, loved us **so, so very much**. He wanted all of us—each and every one of us—to have an intimate, loving relationship with Him, so much so that He was willing to give His most beloved Son and Companion, the Darling of Heaven, Jesus, to suffer horribly at the hands of His own creation in order to satisfy His righteous judgment of sin on behalf of those who would believe. **Of course each of us, having committed sin, deserved to personally receive God's judgment for our sin; but God, who is rich in mercy and love, judged sin on the person of His own dear Son, Jesus, in order that we who believe on Jesus may receive forgiveness of sin from God and go free**. Can we even begin to know and understand what it cost our Father to give His beloved Son and Companion to hang on a cross taking the sin of the world on Himself in order to make a way for us to be "right" or "righteous" in God's eyes through our faith in Jesus? It is the Blood of His own, dear, precious, beloved Son shed for us that makes us right with God. All of God's righteous judgment for sin was placed on Jesus. The entirety of God's wrath was poured out, not on us who deserved it, but on Jesus, His Son, the spotless Lamb of God who did not deserve to be punished. Jesus fully satisfied the requirements of God's punishment for sin so that we do not have to experience anything but God's acceptance and love! How can we fathom that kind of love? And yet, that is the kind of love God has freely bestowed on us in His Son Jesus! Listen, we as humans can only try to understand these things by comparing them to our own limited feelings of love towards those who are dear and precious to us, but God is so infinitely higher, purer and greater than we. How He sees, perceives, feels and is touched is far beyond what we have or could ever know or experience in this body of flesh. The glory of truly knowing and clearly seeing without any hindrance what it cost Him to carry out His plan to save us and bring us to Himself would surely overwhelm our flesh to the point of death could we truly see it. The knowledge, understanding and wisdom of God is far, far beyond the little that we now see and know, and His ability to be touched is far superior to ours for *He is love itself.*

Dearest reader, please consider the great awesomeness and infinity of God. Let us release Him from the small box that we have placed Him in through our small human doctrines and thinking, and accept the true Gospel. There are not words to express what He was willing to suffer in order to bring each of us to Himself and bless us through the Blood of His Son. Jesus is

God's Son according to the Word of God, and He is God's love revealed to us in the flesh.

In the beginning was the Word and the Word was with God. He was in the beginning with God. And the Word was made flesh and dwelt among us. *John 1:1-2, 14*

...(God) has in these last days spoken to us by His Son, whom He has appointed heir of all things, through whom also He made the world; who being the brightness of His glory and the express image of His person. *Hebrews 1:2-3a NKJV*

But God demonstrates His own love for us in this: while we were still sinners, Christ died for us. *Romans 5:8*

The Bible tells us in *Romans 8:32*,

He who did not spare His own Son, but gave Him up for us all—how will He not also, along with Him freely give us all things?

Jesus is God's dearest and best. Jesus is how God chose to lavish His love upon us. The Bible tells us that **God Himself was in Christ reconciling the world to Himself** (*See 2Corinthians 5:19*)! Think of it! It is beyond human comprehension, but the Holy Spirit, our Helper, helps us grasp these awesome truths. **God is not, is not ever—no never—looking for a way to keep us away from or apart from Himself,** but He has done everything in order to bring us close to Himself. God loves each of us so much that He was not willing to live without us, so He died in order that He might make a way to bring us close to Him—into relationship with Him! He has given everything to purchase us, redeem us, cleanse us and bring us to Himself, and has committed Himself wholly and totally to our welfare in this New Covenant which was established in the Blood of His Son.

From the beginning of mankind when Adam and Eve sinned in the Garden of Eden, God began implementing His plan to bring His Son into the earth to shed His Blood in order to justify those who would believe on Him. In *Genesis 3:15* we hear God's words to the serpent who deceived Eve,

And I will put enmity between you and the woman and between your offspring and hers; he will crush your head, and you will strike his heel.

This scripture is prophetically speaking of Jesus who fulfilled it when He was born of a virgin, died on the cross and rose to life again. The devil struck Jesus' heel and injured Him momentarily, but Jesus dealt the death blow to Satan's head by rising from the dead. Jesus took the devil's authority away from him and gave it to us who believe on Him!

And having spoiled principalities and powers, He made a show of them openly, triumphing over them in it. *Colossians 2:15*

...He gave them power and authority to drive out all demons and to cure diseases... *Luke 9:1*

Behold I give you the authority to trample on serpents and scorpions and over all the power of the enemy and nothing shall by any means hurt you. *Luke 10:19 NKJV*

As we continue our study of God's plan written in the Old Testament, we see in *Exodus 20:3-17* that God gave the Law or the Ten Commandments to His people Israel. He did this in order to keep them in some semblance of order, under the tutelage of the Law, until Jesus could come into the earth through Jewish lineage and bring us salvation. God then gave us the Holy Spirit to lead us from the inside out.

Therefore the law was our tutor to bring us to Christ, that we might be justified by faith. But after faith has come, we are no longer under a tutor. *Galatians 3:24-25*

But when the time had fully come, God sent His Son, born of a woman, born under the law, to redeem those under law, that we might receive the full rights of sons. Because you are sons, God sent the Spirit of His Son into our hearts, the Spirit who calls out, "Abba Father". So you are no longer a slave, but a son; and since you are a son, God has made you also an heir.
Galatians 4:4-5

Again in *Isaiah 53:4-12,* we see a prophecy of Jesus as our Savior.

Surely He took up our infirmities and carried our sorrows, yet we considered Him stricken by God, smitten by Him and afflicted. But He was pierced for our transgressions, He was crushed for our iniquities, the punishment that brought us peace was upon Him and by His wounds we are healed. We all, like sheep, have gone astray each of us has turned to his own way; and the Lord has laid on Him the iniquity of us all. He was oppressed and afflicted yet He did not open His mouth; He was led like a lamb to the slaughter, and as a sheep before her shearers is silent, so He did not open His mouth. By oppression and judgment He was taken away, and who can speak of His descendants? For He was cut off from the land of the living for the transgressions of my people He was stricken. He was assigned a grave with the wicked, and with the rich in his death though He had done no violence, nor was any deceit in His mouth. Yet it was the Lord's will to crush Him and cause Him to suffer, and though the Lord makes His life a guilt offering, He will see His offspring and prolong His days, and the will of the Lord will prosper in His hand. After the suffering of His soul, He will see the light of life, and be satisfied; by His knowledge My righteous servant will justify many, and He will bear their iniquities. Therefore I will give Him a portion among the great because He poured out His life unto death and was numbered with the transgressors. For He bore the sin of many and made intercession for the transgressors.

Jeremiah 31:33-34 clearly states God's intention of making a New (and better) Covenant with the human race.

This is the covenant I will make with the house of Israel after that time, declares the Lord. I will put My laws in their minds and write it on their hearts. I will be their God and they will be My people. No longer will a man teach his neighbor or a man his brother, saying, Know the Lord, because they will all know me, from the least of them to the greatest, declares the Lord. **For I will forgive their wickedness and will remember their sins no more.**

God accomplished this through His Son Jesus Christ. Through Jesus we have forgiveness of all our sins, and God says that He has even forgotten all of our sins as well. This forgiveness did not come cheap. We cannot begin to understand the price God paid in order to give us right standing before Him. As we see in *Isaiah 53:10,* it was God's will to crush Jesus and cause Him to suffer. He made Jesus a guilt offering **for us**. Jesus took all our guilt, all of our shame, and God poured out all His righteous judgment and wrath for sin on Jesus. All of our sin was placed on Jesus, and He died with it—paying the price for all sin once and for all. But God raised Him from the dead to new life! He is alive, and through our faith in Jesus we die to a life of sin and are raised to new, eternal life—a life of love—new creations in Christ Jesus. The previously mentioned scripture, *Jeremiah 31:33-34,* is quoted twice in the New Testament book of Hebrews (*Heb. 8:10-12 and Heb.10:16-17*). God is repeating Himself here to make a point. He wants us to know for certain and for sure that He has forgiven all our wickedness and remembers our sins no more! We are told in *Hebrews 9:15* that we have been given a new and better covenant, a New Covenant that is better than the Old Covenant or the Old Testament.

[Christ the Messiah] is therefore the Negotiator and Mediator of an [entirely] new agreement (testament, covenant) so that those who are called and offered it may receive the fulfillment of the promised everlasting inheritance-since a death has taken place which rescues and delivers and redeems them from the transgressions committed under the (old) first agreement.

Hebrews 9:15 (AMP)

This covenant was entered into by God the Father and Jesus, and is therefore eternal and unbreakable because it is impossible for God to lie (*See Hebrews 6:18*). This New Covenant is based on better promises (*See Hebrews 8:6*). Jesus shed His perfect Blood to seal the deal, and we get to participate in and partake of the benefits of this New Covenant through our faith in Jesus! We enter into this New Covenant by believing, not by working. We believe on Jesus and the **work He did** *for us*! What an awesome and loving God who would suffer and experience death, the greatest loss of all, in order to gain back the objects of His love and desire, His beloved creation, mankind!

We are so very blessed and privileged to be the recipients of such great, unshakeable, immeasurable love! Truly, when we enter into Christ, we are enfolded in the "cleft of the rock", standing firm on the foundation of His love for us.

For God did not send His Son into the world to condemn the world, but to save the world through Him. *John 3:17*

The true message of the Gospel of Jesus Christ is the message of forgiveness, love and no condemnation or guilt. The Bible tells us that through the Gospel a righteousness that is from God is revealed. So much of the time the Gospel is presented as a Gospel that focuses on our sin, but that is not what the Bible teaches. **The Bible tells us in *Romans 1:17* that the Gospel—the Good News—reveals a righteousness that is from God.** Truly this is Good News to us! God is not looking at us with eyes that scrutinize us for our sins, faults and unworthiness, but He has completely resolved the sin issue forever through Jesus and is now looking at us with eyes that see us as righteous and worthy of His love through our faith in Christ Jesus alone.

For in the Gospel a righteousness from God is revealed, a righteousness that is by faith from first to last, just as it is written, The righteous will live by faith. *Romans 1:17*

What great love the Father has lavished on us that we should be called children of God! *John 3:1*

God revealed His love for us through the life, death and resurrection of His own Son, Jesus, so that we who place our faith and trust in Him may be made righteous children of God— righteous with God's very own righteousness!

God made Him who had no sin to be sin for us, **so that in Him we might become the righteousness of God.** *2Corinthians 5:21*

Beloved, God loves us **so!** Let us move on and leave the life of sin consciousness behind, entering into His love gift to us—a life of forgiveness and righteousness, the very righteousness of God Himself. God has dealt with sin completely and forever in His Son. Every sin we would ever commit—past, present or future—has been judged in the Body of Jesus Christ, God's gift of love to us. Let us draw near to God through the Blood of Jesus and enjoy the beautiful, abundant life of peace and joy in righteous, loving fellowship with our Heavenly Father!

…for all have sinned and fall short of the glory of God, and **are justified freely by His grace** through the redemption that came by Christ Jesus. God presented Him as a sacrifice of atonement **through faith** in his Blood. *Romans 3:23-25*

Therefore since **we have been justified through faith, we have peace with God** through our Lord Jesus Christ. *Romans 5:1*

Let us rejoice in the gracious words of prophecy which King David spoke in *Psalm 32.* Surely David had felt the judgment of God for his sins with Bathsheba and against Uriah the Hittite. This judgment was the result of his sin under the Old Covenant Law. But David prophetically saw and spoke about a time to come—our time, the time of grace and the New Covenant through Jesus Christ!

Blessed are they whose transgressions are forgiven, whose sins are covered. Blessed is the man whose sin the Lord will never count against him. *Romans 4:7-8*

In studying Jesus as God's love revealed to us, we see in the Gospel of John that John the Baptist had a very graphic description of Jesus and His mission. John the Baptist described Jesus as "the Lamb of God who takes away the sin of the world."

The next day John saw Jesus coming toward him and said, "Look, the Lamb of God, who takes away the sin of the world!"

John 1:29 KJV

In John the Baptist's description of Jesus as the Lamb of God who takes away the sin of the world, he speaks volumes concerning the transition out of the Old Testament and into the New Testament. He is comparing Jesus to an Old Testament (or Old Covenant) animal sacrifice. In the time of the Old Covenant, God's people were living under the supervision of God's Law given to Moses on Mount Sinai. At this time and until the resurrection of Jesus, when a sin was committed it had to be atoned for by the sacrifice of an animal, whether a bull, goat, sheep or even a bird. There were very specific instructions given in the law for these sacrifices depending on who sinned and many other criteria. It was a highly involved process and was continually being repeated over and over. The animal was sacrificed, and its blood was used to make amends for the sin. After the animal was sacrificed properly, the sin would be forgiven. The following is an example of one such command for an animal sacrifice to atone for sin.

If a member of the community sins unintentionally and does what is forbidden in any of the Lord's commands, he is guilty. When he is made aware of the sin he committed, he must bring as his offering for the sin he committed a female goat **without defect** …and he will be forgiven. *Leviticus 4:27-28 & 31b*

In light of this scripture, we see that John the Baptist was telling us (as interpreted by the Word of God in the Old Covenant) that **Jesus is God's very own chosen Lamb**—God's chosen sacrifice, His final sacrifice—for the sin of the whole world. Jesus, God's Son, being fully man, is the only man who ever lived a perfect, sin-free life. Jesus kept God's Law perfectly and completely. He then hung on the cross, voluntarily taking upon Himself the whole burden of every sin that was or would ever be committed in the world. He died a sinner's death thereby satisfying God's righteous judgment on sin once and forever, but rose again to everlasting life—a **perfect sacrifice without defect** for all who believe—the Lamb of God who takes away the sin of the world!

Now returning back to the Old covenant Law, the person who sinned was required to bring a perfect animal to the priest for his sacrificial offering. Let's stop here a minute and think. **The animal being offered must be perfect, without defect.** The person who sinned obviously was not perfect or without defect. This person was flawed by his sin. That is the reason why he must offer a perfect, defect free animal. **It was the animal sacrifice that was examined by the priest, not the person who had sinned**.

In the same way, we as people who sin and need forgiveness from God have a perfect sacrifice to offer for each and every sin we have or ever will commit. Our sacrifice is Jesus, the Lamb of God. He has been chosen, examined and declared the perfect, defect free sacrifice for the sin of the whole world by God Almighty! When we have faith in Jesus and His completed mission of being God's chosen sacrifice, God examines the Lamb of God and sees His perfection on our behalf. God is not expecting perfection of us. Jesus satisfied God's requirement for perfection, and we access perfect and righteous standing with God through our faith in who Jesus is and what He has accomplished for us! Oh what Good News! What a gracious, loving and good God we serve! Out of our love, gratitude and respect for Him, and through the free gift of His grace, we will live upright lives that honor and please our God—not through our own perfection, but through Jesus, the perfect Lamb of God! Jesus has pleased God completely and has utterly destroyed the wall that sin had built between us and God. We, too, please God by our faith in Jesus and His sacrifice for the cleansing of our every sin.

Yes, this is God's love revealed to us, Jesus Christ, through whom we have been given complete and total forgiveness, and peace and fellowship with God! This is the New Covenant, the covenant of God's love and grace to us, sealed in the Blood of His Son, Jesus.

Once we become righteous through our faith in Christ, we are to live our Christian life in relationship with Jesus, who is God's love revealed in us. It is not a hard life of working to please God and scrutinizing ourselves for every wrong-doing and sin. It is not a life of "walking on eggshells" lest we displease God and break fellowship with Him. It is not a life of trying to love God more and trying to prove our love by all of our works. No, no, no! A thousand times, No! Our life of faith **in** Christ pleases God because Jesus has pleased His Father one hundred percent. This Christian life is to be a life of righteousness, peace and joy because we are living out of the overflow of God's love for us given to us in Jesus. We need **only** to **believe** in God's Son, Jesus, and daily receive His cleansing Blood in our lives. There is no way that we are going to stand before God one day and justify ourselves by saying, "Jesus paid it all…and I helped." It is just not going to happen that way. Either we accept that "Jesus paid it all", once and forever; or we are saying that by our works we can make ourselves more acceptable to God. This is not the correct interpretation of New Testament Christianity, and is not pleasing to our Father God because it does not give all the glory and honor to Jesus. Jesus, God's love gift to us, is our one and only plea before God, period. Whatever good works and love flow out of our lives is only a manifestation of His love in us.

Jesus said, "Come unto Me all you who labor and are heavy laden, and I will give you rest. Take My yoke upon you and learn from Me, for I am gentle and humble in heart, and you will find rest for your souls. For My yoke is easy and My burden is light."

Matthew 11:28-30

His yoke is EASY! His burden is LIGHT! Love makes things easy and light. Do our lives reflect easy and light or hard and heavy? Love is the oil that makes our lives run easily and gracefully. Jesus is God's love revealed. As we see this truth and receive His love to empower our lives, we will rest securely in Christ knowing that He has finished the Father's work on the cross and that through Him we are totally accepted and pleasing to God. We will live in light and easy fellowship with Him because He has already accomplished the hard part for us through His love!

Our Father God does not want us to live in fear or with a sense of condemnation over our sins. He has given us His Lamb to be our perfect sacrifice through our faith in Him. By living our lives hidden in Christ, we should feel confident in God's acceptance of us and of His love for us. Consider the following scripture. In *John 8* we read about a woman who was caught in the act of adultery by the teachers of the Law and the Pharisees. They brought her before Jesus and told Jesus that the Law demanded that she be stoned for her offense. They asked Jesus what He had to say concerning this situation

41

because they desired to trap Him by His words. Jesus, in turn, told these men that whoever of them was without sin should throw the first stone at her. One by one they all left, and finally, it was just the adulterous woman and Jesus who remained. In *verse 10* we read,

Jesus straightened up and asked her, Woman, where are they? Has no one condemned you? No one, sir, she said. Then neither do I condemn you, Jesus declared. Go now and leave your life of sin.

Jesus gave this woman a beautiful gift! It is the gift of no condemnation. It is the same gift He has given to you and me. Within this gift lies the amazing grace of God and the ability to go and leave a life of sin, condemnation and guilt. A constant consciousness of our sin will lead to more sin, but the gift of forgiveness and no condemnation sets us free to live a life that leads to holiness and purity. Through the forgiveness and grace we receive in Jesus, we stand firmly planted and rooted in His great love for us.

GOD'S LOVE— OUR CHRISTIAN FOUNDATION

3

I keep asking that the God of our Lord Jesus Christ, the glorious Father, may give you the Spirit of wisdom and revelation so that you may know Him better. *Ephesians 1:17*

Having established in Chapter 1 that "God is Love" *(See 1John 4:8, 16),* we are able to easily see that Paul is praying in *Ephesians 1:17* for the Holy Spirit to give us wisdom and revelation so that we may know God, who is Love, better. The revelation of knowing God as love is the first and foremost revelation that we as Christians should receive according to the Apostle, and every other heavenly insight given to us hinges on this chief and most glorious revelation. As Paul continues in *Ephesians 1:18-23*, he prays that following the revelation of knowing God, or Love, better, we will also know our calling in Him, what our inheritance is in Christ, His great resurrection power operating in our lives, our authority in Jesus and the mystery of the Body of Christ—the Church.

Another of Paul's Spirit inspired prayers for us is in *Ephesians 3:17-19*,

...so that Christ may dwell in your hearts through faith. And I pray that you, being rooted and established in love, may have power together with all the saints, to grasp how wide and long and high and deep is the love of Christ, and to know His love that surpasses knowledge-that you may be filled to the measure of all the fullness of God.

He prays that we would be "rooted and established" in love, and that as we become rooted and grounded in love (God's love for us), we will be able to actually begin to know the dimensions of God's love and even be filled with ALL the fullness of God! What a promise! What a mind-boggling proposition—that we could be filled with all the fullness of God! Reaching this awesome infilling in God hinges completely on our being rooted and established in His love for us.

A clear examination of the words *rooted* and *established* will bring a better understanding of their full meaning. In the Greek language, the language with which the

New Testament was written, the word *rooted* may also be translated *stable, steadfast* or *unmovable*. The word *established* also translates as *grounded* or *to lay the foundation*. It is clear that Paul was praying for us that we would be stable and rooted in love—in God and His love for us—just as a great tree is rooted and stable in the earth. We are told that the root structure of a towering tree is as vast underground as the structure that we see above the ground, and through this system the tree receives its nourishment. The roots of our Christian life must be firmly entrenched and stable in love—in God's love revealed to us through His Son Jesus, in His complete forgiveness and acceptance of us because we have been made righteous through our faith in Jesus. This type of foundation will continually nourish and feed us spiritually, and we will be strong and victorious in our Christian walk.

As we explore the word *established* and its synonym *to lay the foundation*, we are reminded of the process of constructing a building. All, who are familiar with building construction, will know that the setting of the foundation is the most critical part of the building process. All of the super-structure of the building will rest upon the foundation. If the foundation is haphazardly built, the whole structure will be compromised. When stress of any sort, whether it be severe weather, shifting earth or any other harsh circumstance, comes against the building, it will be badly damaged or even destroyed because the foundation, not being solidly built, will be shaken and damaged.

A few years ago, a building project was begun on the corner of our block just up the street from the apartment complex where we were living. Day after day the big earth-movers continued to dig. We were interested in the progress of the project and would check it out as we drove by daily. Months passed by. We kept wondering when the building would begin to go up. The digging and rock removal seemed endless. Then the concrete began being poured, a steady stream of trucks lining up day after day to pour out their contents. Finally, after about one and a half years, the super-structure began to go up, and it went up quickly compared to the digging and laying of the foundation.

Likewise, we as Christians have largely missed the critical importance of laying our Christian foundation in God's great love **for us**. We have glibly mouthed the scriptures, quoting them perfectly, *For God so loved the world that He gave His only begotten Son... John 3:16,* but have rushed headlong into trying to base our Christian lives on how much **we love God,** and then **trying to prove our love for Him by our works**. In building a correct foundation, we must remember that, *"We love God because **He first loved us.**" 1John 4:10;* and that unless we have made God's love *for us* our only foundation in the Christian faith, we have no true love (God's kind of love or agape love) to offer anyone else. We may do some good works, but our motives are not pure, and we are hindered in truly loving others with God's unfailing love. Our works will have their roots in self-righteousness and pride as we try to justify ourselves in God's sight, rather than understanding that Jesus is our only plea and justification before God. God's kind of love can only come from God Himself, and we can only access His love by basing our complete and utter faith in His love for us which is revealed in His Son Jesus and His finished work upon the cross.

Let's use our imaginations to envision ourselves standing on a large slab which would symbolize Jesus, our Rock. Let's see God's love being poured out like concrete all around us. Let's see it cover our shoes, then our ankles, up our calves to our knees and then above our knees. We can then see ourselves standing there, up to our thighs in that concrete for eight hours—standing there until the concrete totally sets up and hardens. At that point we will be stable, fixed and immoveable in the concrete—in God's love for us. Winds and circumstances may blow against us. We may lean a bit, but we will not be blown over because we are fixed in the concrete, the foundation, of God's love; knowing that no matter what, God loves me, and I am right with Him through Jesus Christ!

And we know (understand, recognize, are conscious of, by observation and by experience) and believe (adhere to and put faith in and rely on) the love God cherishes for us. God is love, and he who dwells and continues in love dwells and continues in God, and God dwells and continues in Him. *1John 4:16 (AMP)*

This scripture reveals the basic belief system of the early church believers. They took hold of God's love for them by faith and refused to let it go no matter what. Could our lack of understanding and believing in God's great love for us be the underlying cause of the weakness and ineffectiveness of the Body of Christ today? The early church was an on-fire, bold group of Believers. They were fervent in their love for God and each other, willing to put others before themselves even to the point of doing without in order to help a fellow Believer, which was a great testimony to the unsaved community.

This revelation of God's love for us does not simply fall down on us from Heaven when we become born-again.

There are so many voices trying to coerce us onto the *works treadmill* once we are saved, and we then begin to try to please God by working, instead of realizing that the only way we can please God is by believing in His Son—the Son of His love. Because this teaching of *works* or *practical righteousness* is so prevalent in the Church today, we must make every effort to focus our attention on God's Word which tells us of His love for us. We must take the time to lay a deep, true and firm foundation on knowing and believing God's love for us that will never waiver or fail us. It matters not how long it may take us to lay this solid and unshakeable foundation in our lives, even as the foundation of a building takes a long time to set if there are rocks and challenges to overcome. What matters is that we lay the foundation properly, regardless of how long it may take, so that our Christian lives may be lived as God intended them to be lived—life abundant!

In laying this foundation properly, we must make a clear distinction between the Old and New Testaments (or the Old and New Covenants). The Bible is divided into two main parts which are the Old Testament (or Covenant) and the New Testament (or Covenant). The Old Covenant is a history of mankind and is also a foretelling of the things to come when Jesus would arrive on the scene and finish the Father's work. The Old Covenant tells of God's dealings with mankind from the beginning, and is full of beautiful types and shadows of our coming Savior. It is filled with wonderful promises made by our Father God and fulfilled in Christ, and it is filled with the wisdom of God. In this Covenant God gave men the Ten Commandments, and there was a curse in effect for those who did not keep God's Law. Those who broke the Law of God received His judgment. In the New Testament, the story of God's redemption of mankind through Jesus Christ is told. Jesus is the only living man who ever completely kept and fulfilled God's Law. At the end of His life, He was hung on a cross, took all the sin of the world and the curse that comes as a result of sin upon Himself, and died.

Christ redeemed us from the curse of the law by becoming a curse for us, for it is written: "Cursed is everyone who is hung on a tree." *Galatians 3:13*

But thank God He was raised from the dead! He arose victorious over all sin and the curse. **Through our faith in Christ and our life in Him, God sees us as having fulfilled the Law and as being free from the curse.** There is no curse in the New Covenant! Jesus is the total fulfillment of God's plan to bless mankind.

He is the Mediator of the New and Better Covenant, which is a completely New Covenant and is better than the Old Covenant.

But the ministry Jesus has received is as superior to theirs as the covenant of which He is mediator is superior in the old one and it is founded on better promises. *Hebrews 8:6*

In *Luke 22:20* Jesus took the cup with the wine and said,

"This cup is the New Covenant in My Blood which is poured out for you."

In saying this and by shedding His Blood for mankind, Jesus initiated a New Covenant. This New Covenant fulfilled all the Old Covenant promises. Through our faith in Christ, we are now in a new place with God, no longer subject to the Law of God and the curse. We, as Christians, get into trouble by not discerning between the Old and the New Covenants. Once we are in Christ through faith in Him, we are released from the Old Covenant.

By calling this covenant "new" He has made the first one obsolete... *Hebrews 8:13*

We are no longer subject to laws and regulations or the curse for not obeying the Law. We are free in Christ to be led by the Holy Spirit from the inside out. The Old Covenant promises are still ours, for **all** the promises are Yes and Amen in Christ *(See 2Corinthians 1:20)*, but we have been redeemed from the curse of the Law *(See Galatians 3:13)*. We must, as New Covenant Christians, base our lives solely on Jesus and His finished work! We must leave the Old Testament with its rules and regulations and learn to be led by the Holy Spirit of God who now lives on the inside of us. He will lead us in paths of righteousness or right paths. He will lead us in the way we should go.

This is the covenant I will make with the house of Israel after that time, declares the Lord. I will put my laws in their minds and write them on their hearts. I will be their God and they will be my people. For I will forgive their wickedness and will remember their sins no more. *Hebrews 8:10 & 12*

It is important for us to understand that to the extent we are still committed to and trying to live by the Old Covenant Law, our eyes will be veiled to the New Covenant truth of God's love for us and His amazing grace given to us in Christ alone *(See 2Corinthians 3:13-18)*. We must, as Believers in Christ, look to Him only and to the exclusion of everything else for our salvation. Jesus is the only way to God. Coming to Him to enter into salvation and then trying to continue to live according to the Law will not lift the veil that keeps our eyes from seeing the simple truth of the New Covenant—the truth that God is totally committed to us in Christ, that He loves us without measure, and that He has completely forgiven us, forever! Jesus is God's pristine sacrifice and victorious trophy for all time for all people, and the New Testament way of life is a new and better way than the Old Testament way. This New way had been on God's mind and heart for men since the beginning. It took thousands of years to implement, but now it is reality for all who will believe!

In this New and Better Covenant, we are no longer being judged for our sins. God has given us freedom from sin and condemnation through our faith in Christ. There is only love, peace, joy and rest given to us in Christ in the New Covenant. Making the clear distinction that we have been released from the Old Covenant (The Law or the Ten Commandments) and the curse for disobeying the Law, and have entered into God's love, grace and peace through Christ, will help us immensely in our knowing God as a God of love and making His love for us our Christian foundation.

There is a principle laid out in the Word of God that is very important for us to understand in order to access and flow successfully in the things that are available to us in God's Kingdom. Consider the following scripture:

That if you **confess with your mouth** "Jesus is Lord", and **believe in your heart** that God raised Him from the dead, you will be saved. *Romans 10:9*

In order to be saved, we must **confess** that Jesus is Lord, and we must **believe** in our hearts that God raised Him up from the dead. Confess and believe! Yes, we must confess with our mouths the truths of God's Word, but there is more to it than just giving lip service to the Word of God. We must also **believe in our hearts** the words we are speaking. This means that we must truly be convinced in our souls (our minds), understand what we are saying and believe that it is true for us **personally** in order to receive the fullness of the truth of God's Word. Whether we are believing for salvation, healing, love or any other area, we must be convinced, fully persuaded and believe that it is true for us personally and that we have received it by faith.

And He said to them, be careful what you are hearing. The measure [of thought and study] you give [to the truth you hear] will be the measure [of virtue and knowledge] that comes back to you - and more [besides] will be given to you who hear.

Mark 4:24 (AMP)

In this scripture, Jesus is telling us to be careful what we listen to, and that when we hear a truth, we need to spend time to think on, meditate on and study the truth on which we are focusing, so that we may walk in or apply that truth successfully. It is most imperative for us to first know and discern by the Holy Spirit (who lives in us) that what we are hearing is actually true according to God's Word. Since, in this book, we are teaching on God's love for us, we will focus on the subject of love as it relates to this scripture. It is imperative that the teaching of the Word of God we hear is taught from the foundational truth of *God is Love. (See 1John 4:8, 16)*. If we hear teaching that portrays God as angry at us, allowing judgment and the curse to come on us because we didn't behave well, and not being pleased with us because we are not doing enough, etc., we are not hearing the truth; and not hearing the truth will ultimately undermine our faith in God and His willingness to answer our prayers. Not hearing the true Gospel of God's love for us will hinder our faith and cause it to be inoperative because faith works by love! *(See Galatians 5:6)*. According to Jesus, **we must be careful what we hear.** God is love. God is good. **What we hear must be based on God's love given to us through the finished work of Christ, and His great grace and favor toward us which enable us to be righteous before Him in love.** This is the Bible truth in the New Testament—the New and Better Covenant which is based on better promises! These are truths on which we can build our Christian foundation that will produce love, joy, peace and rest in our lives. These are the truths that we must spend our time thinking about, meditating on and studying in order to live successful Christian lives. In other words, just singing "Jesus loves me this I know" or quoting John 3:16 perfectly, "For God so loved the world..." without spending quality time thinking about and studying God's love for me until **I am convinced in my mind and believe in my heart** that it is a reality for me in my own life, it will not profit me. Lip service alone (or confession alone), without understanding and believing that the truth applies to me *personally,* will not give me the victory in my Christian life. But if I give myself to the study of God's love for me and keep it in the forefront of my thinking day by day, deciding on purpose to believe it and not let it go no matter what circumstances may bring, I will become rooted, stable, fixed and immoveable on my foundation. I will become unshakeable and can build my Christian life securely on this perfect foundation which is God's perfect and unending love for me that was demonstrated through Jesus Christ who has won every victory for me!

Understanding that we must be careful what we hear, as Jesus told us in Mark 4, sheds a new and much needed light on why we, as Christians, need to be planted in a church where we hear the true Gospel of the Lord Jesus Christ preached and taught. It is God's plan for the leaders of the churches to teach Believers the manifold grace of God. It is so important to attend a church where God's love for us is the foundation, and Biblical truths are taught from this foundation of God's love, grace and righteousness. Be careful what you hear! It will make all the difference in whether you walk in God's victory, peace, love, joy and health or in defeat, fear, depression and sickness. It will make all the difference in allowing your faith to flow freely; and the flow of faith is imperative in our Christian lives for,

The just shall live by faith. *Hebrews 10:38*, and ...faith works by love. *Galatians 5:6*.

There is no fear in love. But perfect love drives out fear.
1John 4:18

Fear is the enemy of Christians, and Satan wields it against us skillfully. Each of us has his or her own areas of weakness, and our enemy, the devil, tries his best to exploit us in these areas. He uses condemnation to defeat us by condemning us for our faults. He also uses guilt over our failures, fear of God's displeasure toward us, fear that we haven't done enough and fear that God will not desire to help us in order to destroy our faith. But if we have been firmly established, deeply rooted and stable in the revelation of God's great, great love for us, we will not be moved by the lies of the devil. If we continue studying this subject of God's love for us until we truly live it, breathe it and believe it, we will be unshakeable, immoveable and strong no matter the circumstances. We will turn a deaf ear to the devil's accusations and lies, for we will be consumed with the knowledge of, and faith in, how dearly and perfectly we are loved and forgiven by our Heavenly Father through our faith in the Lord Jesus Christ. We will be convinced that God is on our side and that He will never, ever leave us or forsake us in any way! We will be joyful, peaceful and at rest knowing that the God who created all things loves us, knows us and has totally committed Himself to us through the Blood of Jesus. We will know that God is for us and that no one can be against us and succeed!

There is no fear in love [dread does not exist], but full grown (complete, perfect) love turns fear out of doors and expels every trace of terror. For fear brings with it the thought of punishment and so he who is afraid has not reached the full maturity of love [is not yet grown into love's complete perfection].

1John 4:1(AMP)

I would like to share a wonderful example of this scripture revealed to us by the lives of Jesus' disciples, John and Peter. Both of these disciples were in Jesus' inner circle. They both experienced the same teaching from Jesus and saw all the same miracles on a daily basis for over three years. But there was a huge contrast in their personal experiences with Jesus as we see illustrated in the Bible. In the book of John, which John the apostle wrote, he repeatedly called himself "the disciple whom Jesus loved". Through his words we can see that he believed in, had faith in and relied on the love that Jesus had for him. He saw and believed himself to be the Beloved of God, and he is still referred to as John the Beloved to this day. He named himself "the disciple whom Jesus loved" because this is what he believed. All the disciples spent personal time with Jesus, and yet we see only John taking hold of Jesus' love for him by faith. He made Jesus' love for him the foundation of his life, calling himself "the disciple whom Jesus loved" rather than his given name. **Jesus offered the same love to all the disciples, but John took His love and made it personal. He based his entire identity on it and made it his only foundation.** Whenever we see John with Jesus, he is close to Him, even laying his head upon him at dinner, and **Jesus never pushed him away!** Jesus came as God's love to all mankind, but we must each personally take Him and His love as our very own.

On the other hand, we see Peter making boasts about **how much he loved Jesus**. In *John 13* Jesus was sharing the Passover meal with His disciples just before He was betrayed into the hands of the Jews. Jesus told His disciples that He was leaving them and was giving them final instructions. Peter boldly told Jesus that,

> …I will lay down my life for you. *John 13:37*

He was boasting in his own abilities because of his love for Jesus. As the events of that night unfolded, Jesus was arrested and taken before the Jewish high priest to be tried. Out of the eleven disciples only John and Peter followed Jesus, and because John was known by the high priest, he was allowed entrance into the courtyard and was able to get Peter into the courtyard as well. As they sat around the fire waiting to see what would happen to Jesus, a servant girl asked Peter if he was one of Jesus' disciples, and he denied it. This happened three times. Why did Peter deny association with Jesus? Fear! He was afraid that, through association with Jesus, he would receive punishment and harm. He was afraid, and he failed the very One whom he had just a few hours earlier claimed he would die for. He actually, at that moment, removed himself by his words from being a disciple of Christ. He denied that he was a disciple of Jesus three times. We read in *Mark 14:71* that Peter

...began to call down curses on himself, and he swore to them, I don't know this man you're talking about.

He denied even knowing Jesus. We see that truly he did not know Jesus, for Jesus is the love of God. If Peter had truly known Jesus, he would have known and received God's love for him, and he would have had no fear.

But the "disciple whom Jesus loved" went all the way through the trial and crucifixion with Jesus. He was with Jesus all the way. He was fearless because he knew God's love for him. We even read in *John 19:25-27* that when Jesus was hanging on the cross, He saw His mother, Mary, and John there with Him and spoke to His mother,

"Dear woman, here is your son," and to the disciple, "Here is your mother." From that time on, this disciple took her into his home.

John's revelation of, faith in, and reliance on God's love for him enabled him to overcome fear and show his love for Jesus by going all the way through His suffering with Him, and to even take Jesus' mother as his own.

> This is love: not that we loved God, but that He loved us,
> and sent His Son... *1John 4:10*

John was able to show his love for Jesus all the way through because he had received Jesus' love for him personally and made it his foundation. Peter, on the other hand, who boasted of his love for Jesus without having a revelation of Jesus' great love for him, failed miserably.

What an awesome example of knowing and having faith in and relying on God's love for us! This revelation— this foundation—will make us fearless Christians who are totally unmanageable by the devil! We will walk as the Sons of God, manifesting all the fullness of our Father in the earth, for we will know and be convinced that nothing can separate us from the love that God has for us!

Who shall separate us from the love of Christ? Shall tribulation, or distress, or persecution, or famine, or nakedness, or peril or sword? ...Yet in all these things we are more than conquerors through Him who loved us. For I am persuaded that neither death nor life, nor angels nor principalities nor powers, nor things present nor things to come, nor height nor depth, nor any other created thing, shall be able to separate us form the love of God which is in Christ Jesus our Lord. *Romans 8:35 & 37-39 NKJV*

As we walk in the boldness of knowing God's love for

us, many unbelievers will come to know God through the love of God which flows through us to others. The Church of our Lord Jesus Christ will be an oasis of the love of God which will bring restoration to our cities, towns and counties.

In closing this chapter, within which we have seen the importance of laying the foundation of our Christian lives on God's love for us, I would like to bring one last scripture to our attention.

I in them and You in Me. May they (Christians, Believers) be brought to complete unity to let the world know that You sent Me and **have loved them even as You have loved Me.** *John 17:23*

Chapter 17 of John is the record of Jesus' prayer for Himself, for His disciples and for all Believers just before His crucifixion. What an awesome statement He made concerning God's love for us as Believers! **God loves us even as He loves Jesus! God loves us just like He loves Jesus!** He loves us just as He loves Jesus because through our faith in Jesus we are living IN Jesus now. This is a truth to which we need to give our attention. We would do well to ponder, meditate, think upon and let it completely change our thinking about how God sees us and relates to us. This is a statement of truth that we can truly base our lives as Believers upon.

This is the truth of God's immeasurable love for us. He loves us just as He loves His own dear Son, Jesus, and upon this foundation, we can stand unmoved in our faith in His love and goodness to us forever throughout all eternity!

YOU ARE GOD'S BELOVED IN CHRIST 4

"To the praise of the glory of His grace, wherein He hath made us accepted in the Beloved." *Ephesians 1:6 KJV*

"[So that we might be] to the praise and the commendation of His glorious grace (favor and mercy) which He so freely bestowed on us in the Beloved. *Ephesians 1:6(AMP)*

The Gospel of the Lord Jesus Christ, which is revealed in the New Testament, is truly GOOD NEWS! This Gospel is the revelation of God's great love for us and of the truth that He has made us accepted, favored and greatly loved **in** His Beloved Son, Jesus. Under the Old Covenant that God established with Israel through the Law of Moses, a person was perfected through his or her performance of the Law; and yet no one could ever be perfected in this manner, for no one was ever able to perfectly keep the Law until Jesus. Under the New

Covenant, the New Testament or grace, we are perfected through Jesus' one sacrifice forever as we believe by faith in His finished work upon the cross. In God's eyes, we are as perfect in our born-again Spirit as our perfect sacrifice, Christ Jesus! Through our perfection in Christ, God's Beloved, we also have become God's Beloved sons and daughters!

In this chapter, we will explore the revelation of knowing that we are God's Beloved. We will see the critical importance this revelation plays in our walking in the victory that Christ Jesus purchased for us with His own Blood. Let's begin by examining Jesus' baptism by John the Baptist in *Matthew 3:16-17 NKJV.*

When He had been baptized, Jesus came up immediately from the water; and behold the heavens were opened to Him, and He saw the Spirit of God descending like a dove and alighting upon Him. And suddenly a voice came from heaven, saying, "This is My beloved Son, in whom I am well pleased."

At the time of Jesus' baptism, He was preparing to begin His public ministry. The scriptures tell us He was about thirty years old. There is a tradition in the Jewish culture that symbolizes a son's transition into manhood. This ceremony is performed when the son turns thirty years of age. At this time, the son's father lays his hands on his son and declares that now the son is his equal—a full grown man. On this occasion, he also expresses his pleasure in his son and blesses him. Jesus' baptism is a picture of the fulfillment of this Jewish custom. God is validating Jesus as His very own Beloved Son, His equal, who would bring the Father's grace to the world. God also expressed His pleasure in Jesus during this encounter. God was blessed and excited to have His grace manifesting in the world at long last through Jesus! These were God's fresh, now words to Jesus which strengthened and encouraged Him, "You are My Beloved Son in whom I am well pleased."

Immediately following Jesus' baptism, He was led by the Holy Spirit into the wilderness where He fasted for forty days and was then tempted by the devil. This event is described in *Matthew 4:1-11*. The first of the three temptations the devil brought before Jesus was,

If you are the Son of God, tell these stones to become bread.
Matthew 4:3.

In these words which the devil spoke, we see that he is challenging Jesus to "do" something in order to prove that He is who God had already said He is. In the same way, he tempted Eve to eat of the forbidden tree in the Garden of Eden. The devil told Eve that if she would eat of the forbidden fruit, she would be "like God" (*See Genesis 3:5*). But, in fact, the Word of God tells us that Adam and Eve were already like God because they were created in His image and likeness (*See Gen 1:26*). So then, through these examples, we see that the trap of the devil is to always try to get us to "do" something in order "to acquire" what God has already told us He has given us in Christ. Jesus defeated the devil in this temptation by not "performing to prove", but by simply believing and trusting that what God had said about Him was true. He simply believed that He is God's Beloved Son in whom God is well pleased, and then He quoted the Word of God which applied to His situation. Remember, too, that God called Jesus His Beloved Son **BEFORE** Jesus' ministry began—before He had performed one miracle. God loved Him and was pleased with Him before any of the great works He did during His ministry! He loved Him for who He was. Jesus had loving fellowship with His Father through His growing up years in the carpenter's shop. Jesus fellowshipped with His Father by seeking Him through the knowledge of the scriptures. Jesus fellowshipped with His Father by living out the scriptures in His everyday life. This was pleasing to God. If we are wise, we will follow Jesus' example of living in loving fellowship with our Father by studying and becoming "doers" of His Word. In this way, we will continue to know more about Him (Love) and live successfully as He desires for us. The second observation we make in the devil's words to Jesus is that he is telling Jesus to turn the stones into bread. There is more to these words than meets the eye. If we look at the word *stones* symbolically based on the Old Covenant, we are reminded of the stone tablets on which God wrote the Ten Commandments. In this context, the devil is tempting Jesus to make the Old Covenant Law of Moses bread to feed the spiritual hunger of mankind. In other words, the devil was trying to misdirect Jesus' mission of giving God's grace to mankind. The devil was tempting Him to validate and enforce the Old Covenant Law as man's way to God. Jesus refused to fall prey to the devil's scheme by answering,

Man shall not live by bread alone but by every word that proceedeth out of the mouth of God. *Matthew 4:4 KJV.*

If we examine the word *"word"* which Jesus used here, its actual definition in the Greek language is a "now or flowing, proceeding" word. Jesus is showing us, by example, that He is living by the last word spoken to Him by His Father, God. He is not changing His course. He knows His ministry is to deliver us from the Old Covenant in which the Law and performance was mankind's bread. He knows His mission is to usher us into a New Covenant where the "now" Word of God, spoken and made alive to us every day by the Holy Spirit who lives in us, is our bread. He Himself is living on the last word that He heard His Father say to Him at His baptism. He is living in union and relationship with His Father, and that is His mission. That is what He came to earth make available to us.

The third and final observation we will make concerning the devil's first temptation of Jesus is in his words, "If you are the Son of God..." Of the words God spoke to Jesus at His baptism, there is one word the devil omitted. God called Jesus His *Beloved Son,* but the devil left out the word *Beloved* when he spoke to Jesus. The devil's strategy was to divert Jesus' attention away from being a *Beloved Son* to being only God's Son. The devil will never remind us that we are the Beloved of God because this is the revelation of **God's love for us,** and it defeats the devil **every time**! He doesn't mind us knowing that we are just a "son" or a "daughter" of God. This type of knowledge carries with it the implication that we must measure up or prove ourselves to our Father. But in receiving the revelation of being God's Beloved because we are in Christ, our perfect sacrifice, we are made totally unmanageable by the devil. Contained in this revelation is peace, rest and a firm foundation of stability in our relationship with our Father God. Being God's Beloved is not based on how much we love Him and do for Him. Being God's beloved is based on the truth that He *first loved us*, and in Christ all of our Father's love is revealed and poured out to us.

This is love: not that we loved God, but that He loved us, and sent His Son as an atoning sacrifice for our sins. *1John4:10*

Jesus successfully defeated the devil in every aspect of this temptation. He rested in the "now" word spoken to Him by His Father, believing that what God had said was true. He believed that He is God's Beloved Son in whom His Father is well pleased. He did not succumb to the temptation to try to prove His standing with God through His works or to hold up the Old Covenant Law as our way back to God. He kept His eyes, His mind and heart set on what God had spoken to Him, that He is God's Beloved Son in whom He is well pleased, and He successfully defeated the devil. We, too, will see the same results, successfully defeating the devil in every area of our lives, by standing firm in the revelation that we are God's Beloved children; because, through our faith, we are **in** God's Beloved, Jesus!

As we continue our journey into the revelation that we

are God's Beloved in Christ, let's move on to the Mount of Transfiguration (*See Matthew 17:1-8*). Jesus took Peter, James and John with Him, and they went up a high mountain by themselves. On top of the mountain, He was transfigured before them.

His face shone like the sun, and His clothes became as white as the light. *Matthew 17:2*

Here we see that God is pouring out His glory on His Beloved Son, once again, and is validating Jesus as His very own choice to bring His grace to mankind. In verse 3 we read,

Just then there appeared before them Moses and Elijah, talking with Jesus.

Moses represents the Law, and Elijah represents the Prophets. They had appeared on the mountain with Jesus in order to confirm Jesus' mission of bringing God's grace to the earth and to testify that the Old Covenant of the Law and the Prophets was being superseded by God's awesome plan to send His grace to the earth. In verse 4 we read,

Peter said to Jesus, 'Lord, it is good for us to be here. If You wish I will put up three shelters—one for You, one for Moses and one for Elijah.'

Peter, who did not understand Jesus' purpose and mission, is trying to place Jesus, Moses and Elijah all on the same level. In other words, he was seeing Jesus, the Law and the Prophets as all equally valid. He was mixing the Old with the New, but Jesus had come to make a totally new Covenant with God by shedding His own Blood.

Verse 5, While he was still speaking a bright cloud enveloped them, and a voice from the cloud said, "This is my Beloved Son, with Him I am well pleased. Listen to Him!"

This statement from Jesus' Father, God, is so very precious and meaningful to all of us who believe on Christ Jesus. Once again, as He did at Jesus' baptism, Father God is confirming and validating Jesus as His Beloved Son. He is also saying, again, that He is well pleased with Jesus. What is unique about God's statement here is that He actually interrupted Peter as Peter was laying out his plan to put Jesus, the Law and the Prophets all on the same level. God, who is Creator of Heaven and earth and of all created things, actually interrupted Peter's dialog and spoke, declaring who Jesus is and telling the disciples, *"Listen to Him!"* In other words He was saying, "Don't listen to the Law any longer. Don't listen to the Prophets any longer. Listen to My Beloved Son!" God was telling us all to no longer base our lives on the Old Covenant Law and Prophets, but to listen to Jesus!

For the Law was given through Moses, grace and truth came through Jesus Christ. *John 1:17*

God is telling us to listen to grace and truth, and to discern between the Old Covenant and the New. Jesus came and established a New Covenant with God that is far superior to the Old. We must know what Jesus' mission on earth was and leave the Old Covenant ways in order to embrace this New Covenant, which is Jesus Christ in you, the hope of glory (*See Colossians 1:27*). According to *James 2:8*, the royal law of this New Covenant is love. We first must receive and believe in God's love to and for us, and we then release His love through our lives to others.

Matthew 17:6, When the disciples heard this they fell face down on the ground terrified. But Jesus came and touched them…

Jesus is always God's love reaching out to touch mankind in order to bless them. Jesus' next words are very important words for us because they are the first words He speaks after God told the disciples to, "Listen to Him!" What were Jesus' next words?

"Get up, He said, Don't be afraid!"

God's desire is always to lift us up! "Get up!" Don't stay pushed down and dominated by the devil in fear, depression, guilt, condemnation, sickness, lack or whatever is pushing you down in your life! Get up! He always desires for us to have more revelation of Him and His love for us so that we may get up, prosper and be blessed spirit, soul, body, financially and in our relationships. How do we accomplish this? *"Don't be afraid!"* Jesus said next. If we listen to Jesus, all fear will have to go! He is our Good Shepherd who makes us lie down in green pastures and leads us beside still, restful waters. The shepherd keeps and protects the sheep. They listen to and follow him and are kept in safety. They stay close to their shepherd and are not afraid when they are with him. So it is with us and our Good Shepherd! Fear is our enemy. Fear is of the devil. God sent Jesus, His love gift to us, so we would no longer live in or tolerate fear in our lives,

There is no fear in love. But perfect love drives out fear because fear has to do with punishment. *1John4:18*

As we receive Jesus, who is God's love revealed to us through His grace, we will be set free from fear of punishment because all our sin and well deserved punishment has been placed on Jesus and dealt with completely and forever! We are free from all worry and fear because we are in Christ, our Good Shepherd, who takes care of us! He tells us in *Hebrews 13:5* that He will

NEVER leave us or forsake us! In this great freedom, we are able to progress in our Christian lives from glory to glory. We do not have to fear for Jesus has become our intercessor before God, holding out His perfect Blood as the evidence of our complete forgiveness and acceptance forever! Hallelujah! This is the Good News! This is the Gospel of the Lord Jesus!

> *Matthew 17:8*, When they looked up, they saw no one except Jesus only.

They did not see Moses. They did not see Elijah. They were no longer looking at the Law or the Prophets, but only at grace and truth, Jesus! He is the Light of the world. He is the Grace of God personified. The Bible tells us that,

God was in Christ reconciling the world unto Himself. *2Corinthians 5:19*

The glory of God's plan in Christ supersedes the Old Covenant Law and Prophets! Jesus stands alone as the glory of God bringing grace and truth to the world!

We will now confirm this teaching in one more stunning illustration given in this account of the transfiguration of Jesus. Jesus took Peter, James and John up onto the mountain with Him. Let's take a look at the meaning of these men's names in the Greek and Hebrew. Peter's name means "stone". James (which is the same as Jacob in Hebrew) means "replaced", and John's name means "grace". Now putting it all together we see God's revelation—the "stone" is "replaced" by "grace"! The Old Covenant Law, written on stones, has been replaced by the grace of God given through His Beloved Son, Jesus Christ! This is the Gospel, and for us to believe God's Gospel is most pleasing to Him and most important to us.

From the Mount of Transfiguration, we will move on to the Garden of Gethsemane. Jesus and His disciples had come to the Garden after the last supper. Jesus knew that Judas would betray Him there. When Judas came to Him leading the chief priests, officers of the temple guard and the elders who were going to take Jesus by force, Peter stood by Jesus even defending Him by cutting off the ear of the servant of the high priest. *Peter was totally committed to Jesus and the establishment of His Kingdom on earth* **as Peter imagined it would be in his mind.** He had seen Jesus escape every evil trap that had been set for Him up to this time. And now **Peter thought** it would be no different, but Jesus allowed Himself to be seized by them and taken. Peter was crushed. His dreams were crushed. **He could not understand** or grasp this change of events. **He became totally disappointed and discouraged because he could not understand why things had not gone as he thought they should.** It was in this defeated, discouraged and confused state that Peter followed Jesus into the courtyard of the high priest. He had, during the last supper, declared his great love for and dedication to Jesus. But when it **looked as though all was lost and Peter couldn't understand what had happened, he became fearful and his love and boldness for Jesus failed**. Peter denied Jesus three times which fulfilled Jesus' prophetic word to Peter.

…Most assuredly I say to you, the rooster shall not crow till you have denied Me three times. *John 13:38*

In contrast, we observe John who had a strong revelation of Jesus' love for him. We know that he had this revelation because as he wrote his gospel—the Gospel of John—**he refers to himself as "the disciple whom Jesus loved" five times. It is this revelation of how much he is loved by God that strengthened him through the same time of testing that he and Peter went through together**. John didn't understand what was going on either. I'm sure he was tempted to be (and may have actually felt) fearful, discouraged and disappointed. But **knowing and believing that he was unconditionally loved by Jesus enabled him to trust, and even though** things weren't going the way he wanted them to, he knew everything would be alright. **The knowledge of God's love for him kept John stable and fixed during the time of temptation**—the temptation to give up and run. Because Jesus' love for him promoted trust in John's heart, he did not give in to this temptation. **Knowing that he was loved enabled John to trust in Jesus, trust in God, trust in His Goodness and Love and trust that all would be well.** John was able to be there for Jesus and to go all the way through Jesus' experience on the cross with Him. From the cross Jesus even gave John the responsibility of caring for His mother, Mary, after His death. Contrasting the experiences of these two men gives us a strong and explicit example of how knowing, or not knowing, that we are the Beloved of God in Christ Jesus will help or hinder us when the going gets tough. **Developing a strong revelation of being God's Beloved will enable us to be bold and strong in the face of every challenge or adversity, knowing that all is well because Jesus, who loves me, is faithful!**

As we progress on to the resurrection of Jesus, we hear Jesus speaking to Mary Magdalene soon after He had risen from the dead in *John 20:17,*

Jesus said, "Do not hold on to Me for I have not yet returned to the Father. **Go instead to my brothers and tell them, I am**

returning to *My Father and your Father, to My God and Your God."*

In this awesome scripture, Jesus is revealing a most important truth. This statement is the very heart of our New Covenant relationship with God. Jesus is telling us that He has finished the redeeming work on the cross and is now returning to His Father to present His Blood in Heaven on our behalf. He is becoming our Intercessor before God. He is returning to the Father who had told Jesus that He is His Beloved Son in whom He is well pleased, and **now Jesus tells us that His own Father is now our Father too!** Because of Jesus' finished work on the cross and our faith in His redeeming grace, we have become one with Jesus through His Holy Spirit. And because we are now one with Jesus through our faith in Him, we have also become Beloved by God! Jesus is the first born of many brethren (*See Romans 8:29*). He is the first born, and we have been born-again in Him. We have become God's Beloved sons and daughters in Christ—adopted by God, accepted by God, greatly favored and beloved by God—even as Jesus is the Beloved of His Father!

Jesus, as the Lamb of God, was God's one and only perfect, hand-picked sacrifice for all time. He had established the New Covenant with God in His Blood.

He had finished the work His Father had given Him to do. The picture of this event in the Old Covenant is found in *Genesis 15* when the "Smoking Oven" (God) and "Burning Torch" (pre-incarnate Christ) walked together through the blood of the animal sacrifices that Abraham had split and laid out as instructed by God. This was a type and shadow of the Covenant to come. It was a picture of the New Covenant that God and Jesus entered into together on our behalf. They swore in God's own Blood, released through Christ, that eternal forgiveness and love would forever be to those whose faith is solidly founded in Christ Jesus. This New Covenant, which is established in the Blood of Jesus, can never fail, lose its power or be annulled or altered in any way. Those who place their faith in Christ are forever perfected in their spirit-man and will live with God eternally. So Jesus, as God's Lamb, shed His own perfect Blood, and then, as an eternal priest, He returned to His Father and presented His perfect sacrifice to His Father on our behalf. Once His sacrifice was presented before the Father and accepted, we too became children of God through our faith in Jesus' Blood and what it had accomplished for us. We now have forgiveness of all our sins forever and have been made the righteousness of God in Christ (*See 2Corinthians 5:21*). This is why Jesus was able to say, "Tell them I am returning to My Father and your Father, to My God and your God." He made the way for us! He is the Way, the Truth, and the Life! No one comes to the Father except by Him! (*See John 14:6*).

Jesus told us in *John 17:23*,

I in them and You in me. May they be brought to complete unity to let the world know that You sent me and **have loved them even as You have loved Me.**

and again in *John 17:26*,

I have made You known to them, and will continue to make You known in order that **the love You have for Me may be in them** and that I Myself may be in them.

Jesus is telling us beyond question that His Father and our Father, God, loves us with just the same love He has for Jesus! We are the Beloved of God through our faith and relationship with Jesus Christ. Jesus made the way for us with His Blood and now we can rest secure in Him knowing that we are much beloved by our Father. That's why Jesus came, and He completely accomplished and finished His mission!

In studying the New Testament (or we can use the term the New Covenant) which was finalized in the Body and

Blood of Jesus Christ, we see (especially in the epistles that John wrote—1,2,3 John) that John referred to Believers in Christ as *Beloved*. Because John had such a great, firm and strong revelation of being the beloved of God, he is telling us that we, as believers in Christ, are God's beloved as well. John knows that this privileged position is valid for every Believer in Christ. He saw himself as God's beloved, and in his eyes, every Christian is the beloved of God. In fact, many of the promises made in his epistles are actually based upon us having knowledge of being God's Beloved. For example, *3John2*,

> Beloved, I pray that you may prosper and be in health even as your soul prospers.

We see in this scripture that our soul (which is our mind, will and emotions) prospers and flourishes to the extent that we know we are the beloved of God in Christ. As our soul prospers, the result will be health in our bodies and prosperity and blessing in every other aspect of our lives.

Again in *3John11*,

> Beloved do not imitate evil but imitate good…

Here it is clear that as we develop a strong, clear revelation that we are God's beloved, we will be empowered to imitate our Father who is good. Imitating our Father, who is good, will become doable for us; for we will know that we are right with Him, accepted by Him and loved and cherished by Him. Having the knowledge of His love for us empowers us to draw near and "be" like Him—imitating Him as a little child imitates his loving Father.

Therefore be imitators of God [copy Him and follow His example] as *well-beloved* children [imitate their Father]. *Ephesians 5:1(AMP)*

Again, we see that knowing we are well-beloved of our Father empowers us to imitate Him by loving others with His love. Living a life that exhibits God's love toward others is a life that exemplifies the royal law of the New Covenant—the royal law of Love! *(See James 2:8)* This love is the law of the New Covenant. It is the atmosphere of Heaven and the essence of who God is. As we live in His love and imitate Him, His Kingdom will be established in our sphere of influence on earth as it is in Heaven!

Our Father in heaven, hallowed be Your Name, Your kingdom come, **Your will be done on earth as it is in heaven.**

Matthew 6:9-10

LIVING A LIFE OF LOVE **5**

Using the Book of Ephesians as a model of God's will for our lives as Christians, we can begin to understand how to join in and partake of Paul's revelation of living a strong victorious life in Christ. His revelation, the first part of which he expounds in *Ephesians chapters 1-3*, is that our Christian lives must be founded and established on each of us having a revelation of God's great love for us individually. The second part of his revelation is that we then live a life of love toward God and others by allowing the love which we have **received from Him to flow out from us** freely; and these truths are stated in *Ephesians chapters 4-6*.

Let's read once again *Ephesians 3:17-19*, but this time from the Amplified version of the Bible.

May Christ through your faith [actually] dwell (settle down, abide, make His permanent home) in your hearts! May you be **rooted**

deep in love and founded securely on love, that you may **have power and be strong to apprehend and grasp with all the saints [God's devoted people, the experience of that love] what is the breadth and length and height and depth of it. [That you may really come] to know [practically, through experience for yourselves] the love of Christ,** which far surpasses mere knowledge [without experience] that you may be filled [through all your being] unto all the fullness of God [may have the richest measure of the divine Presence and become a body wholly filled and flooded with God Himself]! (AMP)

As humans we live in a world that generally operates on the *no mercy* principle. Its philosophy is, "Do whatever you can to get all you can, then *can* all you get and sit on the can." It is a philosophy that is *all about me and mine.* The attitudes that we absorb from the world tend to harden our hearts, and even though we become born-again Christians and have been taken out of the kingdom of darkness and placed into the kingdom of light through our faith in Jesus, we must allow the knowledge of God's love for us to soften the hardness of our hearts by renewing our minds to this great love. God's agape, supernatural love is in direct opposition to the world's concepts of love. As we meditate on, focus on, think about and make God's love for us our priority, we will be changed and begin to think and act like our Father God. Since we have received so much love and forgiveness from God, we will want to be merciful and forgiving toward others.

As we follow after knowing God (who is Love) and allow His love for us to engulf us and melt our hardened hearts, we will begin to fulfill the scripture Paul relates to us in *Ephesians 5:1-2(AMP)*,

Therefore be imitators of God *(*who is love)* [copy Him and follow His example] as well-beloved children [imitate their father]. And **walk in love [esteeming and delighting in one another] as Christ loved us and gave Himself up for us**, a slain offering and a sacrifice to God [for you, so that it became] a sweet fragrance. **my personal note*

To be quite honest it is impossible to truly live a life that imitates God unless we have first begun to understand and receive His fathomless love for us. It is by meditating on, yielding to and receiving His love for us that we will be empowered in our hearts to release His same kind of agape love to others. Not having our lives built on, rooted in and established in His true love for us is the telling reason that we Christians have not effectively shown God's love to the world—much less to each other in the Body of Christ. This love is not of the world or of natural human origin. It is not innate to us as human beings. It is a supernatural, Heavenly love and may only be released out of us as it is received by us from our Heavenly Father. Jesus said in *John 13:34,*

"A new commandment I give you. Love one another. As I have loved you, so you must love one another. By this all men will know that you are my disciples, if you love one another."

In other words, Jesus is telling us that exhibiting God's kind of love (agape) in our lives is the distinguishing mark or characteristic of a Christian (one who believes in and receives Christ and His finished work on the cross). Jesus said that if we love one another *as He has loved us* (with the same kind of love He has for us or in the same way He has loved us) the world will know that we are disciples of Christ and be able to distinguish us from non-believers. In considering this scripture, we must realize that we cannot love others as He has loved us unless we first know and experience His love for us. His love will always distinguish us from non-believers. We look for distinguishing marks on natural objects in the world. For instance, an apple tree is distinguished as being an apple tree by the fruit it bears—apples! A pair of Nike shoes is distinguished as being Nike by the "swoosh" emblem on the side. A bluebird is distinguished as such by it song, its blue color and orange breast. A Christian is distinguished as being a Christian by the unselfish, God kind of Heavenly, agape love he or she exhibits in their lives. Many times if we find a plant that we are unable to identify, we need only wait until it bears flower or fruit in order to positively identify it. The same is true concerning Christians. A person may tell us that they are a Christian, but as time passes we see by the fruit of their lives that they truly do not know God (*Love*) or have His love shed abroad in their hearts. The distinguishing mark of being a Christian is walking in Christ-like love toward others because we have received this love without measure from Him!

We know that as Believers in Christ we have been given His love according to *Romans 5:5,*

And hope does not disappoint us, because God has poured out His love into our hearts by the Holy Spirit whom He has given us.

Walking in Christ-like love is a process in which we continually grow, and we each fall and fail many times as we travel our individual paths in Christ. But because our Heavenly Father loves us so very much, He has given us Jesus who has completely paid the price for our failures and sins. He has given us a precious gift—the gift of complete forgiveness each and every day (*See Psalm 103:3*). Each and every day He is looking at us with eyes of love and remembers our sins no more because of the Blood of Jesus. *Our goal should always be to grow more and more like Christ every day, and by so doing to honor our Heavenly Father and to serve Him fervently out of our love and gratitude for all He has done for us! We love Him because He first loved us, and we should desire to live lives that honor Him in every way. We do not want to hurt Him or dishonor Him by doing evil or sinning any longer. We do not desire to sin any longer for we have been made into new creations through our new birth in Christ.*

Therefore, if anyone is in Christ, he is a new creation; old things have passed away: behold all things have become new.

2Corinthians 5:17 NKJV

Yes, we all will fail from time to time—probably daily in some way or another—but Jesus has made provision for that through His Blood. *The motive of our hearts as Christians is to do right and honor God*, therefore we accept His gift of forgiveness daily and ask Him to help us and change us more and more into Christ-likeness. It is much like a love relationship that we might have on earth with a beloved spouse or a parent-child relationship. We may deeply and sincerely love that person, but from time to time we say or do the wrong thing and unwittingly cause them pain. Ideally, we would then ask for and be granted forgiveness and move on in our love relationship with each other. Because we love them deeply, our motive is to never do anything that would hurt, shame, dishonor or tear them down. Even so, in loving God because He first loved us, we should always desire to bless, serve and honor Him and to always represent Him well by walking according to His Word. The Bible tells us that when we love others we are pleasing our Father. And this is not a hard or grievous thing for us to do because when we truly are in a love relationship with someone, we do not have to *make* ourselves do what is right and good towards them. What is right and good flows easily out of us to them because of the love we have for them. We delight to do good to and for them. As we cultivate and grow in our love relationship with our Heavenly Father, we will delight in walking uprightly and righteously before Him—honoring Him with our lives as we receive all He has so freely given us in Christ.

We have been declared righteous by God through our faith in Christ. Our faith in the grace given to us through Jesus gives us victory over sin in our lives.

…for sin shall not have dominion over you, for you are not under law but under grace. *Romans 6:14 NKJV*

We progressively grow in Christ-like behavior as we continue to live in Him and in His Word, receiving His love, forgiveness, acceptance and grace hour by hour. We will begin to exhibit righteous behavior out of our love relationship with Christ who has made us righteous by His Blood—not because we are "trying to" or "compelled to" keep a list of rules in order to please God or because we think our good works are earning us "points" with God. **We could *do nothing* to save ourselves from Hell except to believe on Christ, and we can *do nothing* to keep ourselves in Christ except to believe.** This Gospel—this Good News—is by faith from first to last. We live by faith in what Jesus has done for us, and through His love for us our lives are impacted and changed. As His love changes us and makes our hearts more and more pliable, we will begin to imitate Him by letting His love flow out of us to others. This is the fruit that is produced in our lives by living in the light of His love, watered by His Word and warmed and filled by His Holy Spirit.

We see, then, that good works (or the releasing of His love out of us) should flow out by our revelation of how much we are loved by our Father. Because His love in us is so powerful and real, it must be expressed outwardly. We want others to be as blessed as we are, and this motivates us to give them the Father's love that is in us! This is the supernatural kind of love that loves others in spite of their unlovely actions toward us. This is the God kind of love that looks past all the junk and failures in other's lives and desires to bless them with God's love!

We can do good works out of obligation, fear, self-righteousness or pride, but good works that are not birthed out of agape love (God's supernatural love) are not empowered by God's Spirit, and they come to nothing.

1 Corinthians 13:1-3, If I speak in the tongues of men and angels, but have not love, I am only a resounding gong or a clanging cymbal. If I have the gift of prophecy and can fathom all mysteries and all knowledge, and if I have faith that can move mountains, but have not love, I am nothing. If I give all I possess to the poor and surrender my body to the flames, but have not love, I gain nothing.

Here the Bible tells us that we can do many *good things*, but if we are not motivated to do them by God's love in us for others, they all come to nothing. Motives become very important in the light of God's Word. Are we doing the things we are doing to try to gain God's approval or because we truly care about others? Do we want to appear *good*, *spiritual* or *important* in the eyes of others, or do we really desire to love and help other people? Are we afraid that if we don't do these *good works* we will be found lacking when we stand before God in the final day? If that is our motivation, we are doing good works motivated by self, selfishness and fear. Beloved, the only way to live a life of love is to bask in, receive and have knowledge of how much we are loved by our Father.

1John 4:18, But perfect love drives out fear.

Knowing that we are accepted by God because of our faith in Jesus *alone* will cause fear to have no place in us. We don't have to work to please God because Jesus finished the work and pleased His Father. Now *through our faith in Christ alone* we are pleasing to God, and as our hearts are tendered in His presence, His love will flow like a mighty river out of us to others. Forgiveness will flow. Patience and joy will flow. Kindness and good manners will flow. Selflessness and peace will flow. Trust, faithfulness, encouragement and hope will flow. Our love toward others will never fail because love (or God) never fails. He will never fail to fill us with all we need in order to overflow with His love if we will continue to seek and live in Him, receiving his love continually and growing in it daily. When we begin feeling out of sorts, we simply need to go to our Heavenly Father for a *fill up*. No matter how long we walk with God, we will always be needy of Him—needing His love, grace and mercy on a daily basis—for without Him we can do nothing!

1 Corinthians 13:4-8 (AMP), "Love endures long and is patient and kind; love never is envious nor boils over with jealousy; is not boastful or vainglorious, does not display itself haughtily. It is not conceited—arrogant and inflated with pride; it is not rude (unmannerly), and does not act unbecomingly. Love [God's love in us] does not insist on its own rights or its own way, for it is not self-seeking; it is not touchy or fretful or resentful; it takes no account of the evil done to it—pays no attention to a suffered wrong. It does not rejoice at injustice and *unrighteousness, but rejoices when right and truth prevail. Love bears up under anything and everything that comes, is ever ready to believe the best of every person, its hopes are fadeless under all circumstances and it endures everything [without weakening]. Love never fails-never fades out or becomes obsolete or comes to an end...*

Our love toward others will never fail to hit the mark as long as it is motivated out of our love relationship with God, and as we have studied in Chapter 1 of this book, God is love. *1Corinthians 13:4-8* defines the fruit of His love toward us and in us through Christ.

Jesus came to make a way for us to return to the Father's love in our lives so that we could be changed into vessels of His love on the earth. Love is the entirety of Christ's finished work. Love is the one commandment of Jesus and the complete fulfillment of the Old Covenant Law.

Love does no harm to a neighbor; therefore **love is the fulfillment of the law**. *Romans 13:10*

Living a life that is motivated by the love that we receive from God through the gift of His Holy Spirit and passing it on to others is the sum total of the New Covenant (or New Testament) way of life. Showing forth God's agape love in the earth is revealing God to the world—for He is love! As New Covenant Believers this is our calling—this is our mission.

In the New Testament there are a multitude of references which speak of loving the brethren—our fellow-Believers in Christ. In his epistles, Paul is continually praising the churches for the love he has heard they have and show to one another.

One scripture, found in *Galatians 6:10(AMP)*, is particularly significant in its message to us.

So then, as occasion and opportunity open up to us, **let us do good** [morally] **to all people** [not only being useful or profitable to them, but also doing what is for their spiritual good and advantage.] Be mindful to be a blessing, <u>**especially**</u> **to those of the household of faith [those who belong to God's family with you, the believers].**

This verse is important to us because it states the need for us to walk in love towards all people (unbelievers). The agape love that we show unbelievers, as we have opportunity, will be a witness to them that God loves them. They will see God's grace, mercy and love through us. But Paul is not simply emphasizing ministering to the lost which is often so much of our focus in the church. Paul goes on to tell us that we need to be mindful or focused on being a blessing—but especially being a blessing to the family of God, the Believers. Many times in the church we place our focus on unbelievers. Paul tells us to do good to the unbelievers, but **especially** to be focused and mindful to be a blessing to our brothers and sisters in Christ.

Thinking and meditating on this verse, I began to see it in light of Christ's prayer before His crucifixion in *John 17:21-23(AMP)*,

That they all may be one, [just] as You, Father, are in Me and I in You, that they also may be one in Us, **so that the world may believe and be convinced that You have sent Me.** I have given to them the glory and honor which You have given Me, that they may be one [even] as we are one; I in them and You in Me, in order that they may become one and perfectly united, **that the world may know and [definitely] recognize that You sent Me and that You have loved them [even] as You have loved Me.**

If we read these verses together with Paul's many admonitions to love the brethren—to love each other fervently, sincerely and devotedly—perhaps we can understand Paul's reason for such admonishments. Could it be as Jesus prayed, that when the world (the unbelievers) sees Believers loving each other in word and deed sincerely, devotedly and living together caring for each other in loving unity; then the unbelievers will know and be convinced that God sent Jesus and that He loves them too? Precious reader, it is important to do good and be a blessing to unbelievers as we have opportunity to do so, but its importance should come only second to how we love and bless and care for our own—our brothers and sisters in Christ. For as Jesus prayed, only in seeing how we speak of and treat each other within the Christian community, the Church, will the world be convinced that God sent Jesus and that He loves them too. Seeing us aggressively loving and caring for and about each other will convince them that God is real, that He is love, and they will want to be a part of that kind of love!

We don't have to look far to see that we as the Church of our Lord Jesus have definitely missed it in this area of love. So often we judge, criticize, gossip about and generally mistreat our brothers and sisters in Christ— especially when they fall or fail in some way. As food for thought, consider the newly born church that we see in the Book of Acts. These Believers were actually selling some of their properties and possessions in order to bring the money and have it distributed to the Believers who had need. This is definitely a departure from modern Christianity! We should be caring toward each other. As we allow God's love to overtake us more and more, we will excel in demonstrating this kind of love for our brothers and sisters in Christ, being motivated by the Holy Spirit from within. This type of love gets the attention of unbelievers because it is so foreign to the world's way of operating. Jesus knew that this is how unbelievers would be impacted for Christ. We, the 21st century Church, have many new frontiers to conquer in these areas of love. It is so exciting to know that as we believe, soak in, and receive God's great, great love for us, we will begin to release it toward each other in the family of God—building up, encouraging, speaking well of, helping and blessing each other in whatever particular needs arise. There is no limit where God will take the church that is built on this kind of love! It will be as Heaven on earth—God's Kingdom come! The family of God is not just our own particular church, but all Believers in all the different parts of the Body of Christ. The love of God breaks through and breaks down barriers of denominations and differences of opinion and prejudices. The Blood of our Lord Jesus Christ and our faith in Him are our only criteria and our common ground as Believers. As we make God's love for us our foundation and stand firm on it, we will, out of the overflow of His love in us, be a blessing to all—but especially to our own, our brothers and sisters in Christ. This love will revolutionize our churches and produce and awesome effect on unbelievers, our cities and our nation!

In closing this chapter, I would be neglectful if I did not relate the role of the Holy Spirit in releasing God's love in us, for without Him nothing works as God intended it to work!

Such hope never disappoints or deludes or shames us for God's love has been poured out in our hearts **through the Holy Spirit who has been given to us.** *Romans 5:5(AMP)*

To the end that through [their receiving] Christ Jesus, the blessing [promised] to Abraham might come upon the Gentiles, **so that we through faith might [all] receive [the realization of] the promise of the [Holy] Spirit.** *Galatians 3:14(AMP)*

Soon after I had my experience with Jesus and became born-again, I began to desire to attend church and fellowship with other Believers. I attended a "house church" that was meeting in my town. It was a wonderful experience, singing praise songs to the accompaniment of the acoustic guitar and hearing the preaching of the

Word of God. One Sunday our pastor began speaking on *1Corinthians 12* and the gifts of the Holy Spirit. He spoke on each gift, and the last one he expounded on was speaking in other tongues. I had heard of speaking in tongues, but I was very "put off" by it. I was frightened of this manifestation of the Holy Spirit. I didn't understand tongues and did not want any part of it! As my pastor spoke, though, I found myself listening intently to try to learn and understand more about this gift that seemed so odd to me. Our pastor closed his message by telling us that if we thought speaking in tongues was wrong, we would have to think he was wrong because he spoke in tongues himself! This was shocking news to me! I really trusted and respected this man. He was low key, sincere and loving—not at all weird or nutty. As I stood joined hand in hand in the circle of Believers at the end of the service, I prayed to my Father, "Father if this is a gift that You want me to have, I will take it." Later in the week as I was spending time in worship and prayer, I became overcome with a great surge of love for Jesus and my Heavenly Father and said, "Father, I don't have the words to tell You how much I love You!" At that moment I was baptized in the Holy Spirit and received the gift of tongues. What a surprising moment that was! And, oh, what joy flooded my soul! This, I realized was the language of God—the language of love!

What I came to understand as time went on is that being baptized in the Holy Spirit, with the evidence of that baptism being speaking in other tongues, is for every Believer. In fact, this wonderful gift was promised to us by Jesus.

But I tell you the truth: It is for your good that I am going away. Unless I go away the Counselor (the Holy Spirit) will not come to you; but if I go, I will send Him to you. *John 16:7*

And I (Jesus) will ask the Father, and He will give you another Counselor to be with you forever—the Spirit of truth (the Holy Spirit). *John 14:16*

…but wait for the gift my Father promised, which you have heard Me speak about. For John baptized with water, but in a few days you will be baptized with the Holy Spirit. *Acts 1:4-5*

But you will receive power when the Holy Spirit comes on you, and you will be My witnesses… *Acts 1:8*

These are four scriptures which definitely tell us that Jesus promised to give us the Holy Spirit after He ascended back to the Father following His death, burial and resurrection. In *Acts 1:8,* we are told that not only will the Holy Spirit come, but that we would receive power as a result of Him coming upon us. Let's look at another scripture in *Acts 2.*

When the day of Pentecost came they were all together in one place. Suddenly a sound like the blowing of a violent wind came from Heaven and filled the whole house where they were sitting. They saw what seemed to be tongues of fire that separated and came to rest on each of them. All of them were filled with the Holy Spirit and began to speak in other tongues as the Spirit enabled them. *Acts 2:1-4*

We also read in *Acts 19* that Paul met some Believers in Christ in Ephesus and questioned them concerning their baptism. Paul baptized them in the Name of Jesus.

After this he placed his hands on them, the Holy Spirit came on them and they spoke in tongues. *Acts 19:6*

In reading the Book of Acts, we see that following the fullness of the Holy Spirit coming upon the Believers lives, the supernatural power of God began to flow— even the supernatural love of God flowing out of them towards each other as Believers in Christ! The Holy Spirit comes into us at the New Birth and seals us unto God.

In Him you also trusted, after you heard the word of truth, the gospel of your salvation in whom also, having believed, you were sealed with the Holy Spirit of promise... *Ephesians 1:13 NKJV*

And when we receive the Baptism into the Holy Spirit, He is released into our lives in a supernatural flowing.

Jesus stood and cried out, saying, "If anyone thirsts, let him come to Me and drink. He who believes in Me, as the Scripture has said, out of his belly will flow rivers of living water." **But this He spoke concerning the Spirit whom those believing in Him would receive:** for the Holy Spirit was not yet given because Jesus was not yet glorified. *John 7:37-39 KJV*

So we see in the previous scriptures that being sealed with the Holy Spirit happens at the time of our salvation, but Jesus said that there is also a receiving of an infilling of the Holy Spirit which is a separate experience from our salvation. In *Acts 19:1-7,* Paul proves to us that receiving the infilling of the Holy Spirit is a separate experience following salvation; for these men had previously been saved, but they had not heard of the Holy Spirit baptism until Paul told them about it. He then laid hands on them and they received this baptism.

Peter recognized in *Acts 2:14-21* that this outpouring of the Holy Spirit, as evidenced by speaking in other tongues, is the fulfillment of the scripture written in *Joel 2:28-32.* It has become a common practice in the modern church to disqualify Believers from receiving this gift that Jesus promised us. This disqualification is perpetrated by the misconceptions and the doctrines of men which say that the baptism into the Holy Spirit was only for Jesus' disciples or for the early church and has since passed away. Some key scriptures that would persuade and prove to us that this type of thinking is totally erroneous and contrary to the Word of God would be the following:

Jesus Christ is the same yesterday, today and forever. *Hebrews 13:8*

For all the promises of God in Him are "Yes", and in Him "Amen" to the glory of God through us. *1 Corinthians 1:20*

The grass withers and the flower fades, but the Word of our God stands forever. *Isaiah 40:8*

Heaven and earth will pass away, but My (Jesus') words will never pass away. *Luke 21:33*

In other words, **Jesus and His words NEVER change**, and **every promise that God has made is "Yes and Amen!" and confirmed in Christ**. The words God has spoken will stand and be valid forever! There is and can never be any valid reason to disqualify a promise made by God in Jesus! If we follow the erroneous logic that the Holy Spirit baptism was only for the disciples and the early church, then we are also in danger of not being able to be saved, or born-again, because who is to say that salvation didn't pass away as well? If we decide to nullify one promise of God, then, to us, every other promise is on shaky ground as well. Believers throughout the centuries, until and including this present day, have received this awesome outpouring of the Holy Spirit, and as **Jesus told us** in *Mark 16:17*, they have spoken in new tongues.

And these signs will follow those who believe: In My name they will cast out demons; **they will speak with new tongues**;

Mark 16:17 NKJV

These are the words, the promise, of Jesus and it is just as valid today as it was for the first century church! This Holy Spirit baptism is God's will for every Believer who will believe and ask for it!

Our brother in the faith, the Apostle Paul, who had one of the greatest revelations of God's love in the early church, said that he spoke in tongues *"more than you all"* (*See 1Corinthians 14:18*). He also had extremely dire circumstances to walk through in his life as a Christian. He knew the importance of the role the Holy Spirit plays in keeping us in the love of God, and he exercised this gift more than anyone else of his era in order to walk in continuous victory!

The infilling of the Holy Spirit and the manifestation of it—speaking in tongues—is a critically important portion of our Christian heritage, and should be a part of our Christian experience. God knew that we needed this baptism. The Holy Spirit is our supernatural inheritance from God. This infilling enables us to walk in the fullness of God (or Love). God (or Love) gave us the Holy Spirit baptism and the gift of tongues because He knew it is a supernatural part of Him that we desperately need! In studying the Book of Acts and seeing the love that the Believers walked in, not only toward the unsaved, but much more toward each other, we can begin to put together the pieces of the puzzle that will reveal to us how this love could be so real and so sincerely and extravagantly expressed. The **first piece of the puzzle is that they believed on Christ.** Then, based on the command of Jesus, they waited for the gift that the Father had promised and **received the Baptism in the Holy Spirit** with the gift of speaking in tongues. In *1John 4*, John the Beloved, the disciple whom Jesus loved, writes what was taught as solid first century church doctrine.

In this is love: not that we loved God, but that He loved us and sent His Son to be the propitiation (the atoning sacrifice) for our sins. Beloved, if God loved us so [very much] we also ought to love one another. If we love one another, God abides in us and His love (that love which is essentially His) is brought to completion (to its full maturity, runs its full course, is perfected) in us! ...And we know and believe and have faith in and rely on the love God has for us. God is love and he who dwells and continues in love dwells and continues in Him. In this [union and communion with Him] love is brought to completion and attains perfection with us... *1John 4:10-12, 16-17 (AMP)*

And again in *Jude verses 20-21,*

But you, beloved, build yourselves up on your most holy faith praying in the Holy Spirit: keeping yourselves in the love of God...

And now we have the full picture. The first Believers in Christ followed Jesus' instructions and waited to receive the gift the Father would send. They were baptized in the Holy Spirit and spoke in other tongues just as Jesus said they would in *Mark 16.* These Holy Spirit filled Believers based their love for God on the truth that they loved Him **because He first loved them.** They **believed in, had faith in and relied on the great love God had for them.** They knew that no matter what was happening, God loved them, and that **if God loved them so very much they ought also to love each other unconditionally.** They knew that the great gift, our inheritance in Christ—the Holy Spirit—was the key to having God's love perfected in them, for the fruit of having the Spirit is love. They built themselves up and kept themselves in the love of God by praying in their Holy Spirit language, tongues. These were the keys to their love walk. The supernatural love of God flowed out of them to others, giving them the desire to give of their abundance to make sure the needs of all the Believers were met! Wow! This is the work of the Holy Spirit within us. The fruit of the Spirit—the result of having Him reside in us—is love. This is the true life of Christ in us, being baptized into His love and led by the Holy Spirit of love from within our hearts. He gives us the desire to express His love, and it is very exciting to see how this love is expressed so uniquely through each individual Believer. Just as God is supernaturally multifaceted, so is His Body, the Church of the Lord Jesus. What a marvelous sight it will be to see the Body of Christ operating in the fullness of God's love for us with each of us expressing our part of His love and bringing great glory to God! One may be called to cook meals to give to needy ones, and another may express God's love by teaching the truth of the Gospel of Christ. One may meet the need of brother in Christ who has lost his job and needs assistance in making his rent or house payment. Another may clean a home for someone who has been ill, and on and on in a never ending circle of love expressed as the Holy Spirit leads each one of us from within our hearts. There is no act of love prompted by the Holy Spirit that is too small to be greatly effective. Beloved, to live a life of love is to truly live the life of God! What a joy! What a delight as we make our way up the "high-way" to Heaven. This is the life we are called to live as Christians— basing our Christian experience on God's love for us by believing in, relying on and having faith in His love for us, and by yielding to and allowing the Holy Spirit to express that love through us to others. This is the New Covenant (New Testament) in His Blood. This is the New Covenant of Love. Of course there will always be challenges to overcome as we live in love with each other. We are each very different and unique individuals, and at times, those differences in others may grate and grind on us. In focusing on each other's good qualities and celebrating the uniqueness of each Believer, we will learn to value and love even those who are very different from us. Pair this valuing of each person together with generous amounts of forgiveness, and we will be in position to walk whole-heartedly in God's love toward others (*See Matthew18:21-22*). Because we know how much we have been forgiven by our gracious Heavenly Father, we will forgive others. No, they may not deserve our forgiveness, but neither did we deserve God's mercy, grace and forgiveness toward us. By imitating our Father in this way, we will see the Holy Spirit bring a smoothness, grace, peace and unity to us in our relationships with each other in the Body of Christ. This will bring much joy to our Father, just as it makes us as parents very happy when our children dwell together in peace and love. Living in His love will bring great glory to our God, for this is the life Jesus died to give us. Let us make His love our focus and highest aim. There is no higher calling! Love never fails and neither will we fail when our lives are built on His love for us and focused on expressing that love as we are given opportunities! We will be patient and kind. We will not be touchy, fretful or resentful. We will not be self-seeking, but seeking the good of others. We will not be jealous or rude or proud or conceited. We will not insist on our own way. We will be giving and forgiving because, according to *1Peter 4:8*, love covers a multitude of sins just as Christ has forgiven us of all our sins. We will begin to imitate and look more and more like our awesome Father, each of us bringing Heaven down to our sphere of influence in the earth! We will be filled and overflowing with all the fullness of God, our Father, as we are rooted and established in His love for us through Christ Jesus our Lord. Our Father loves us because we have chosen to believe in His Son Jesus, not because of our good works. But because we are in Christ Jesus and His Spirit is in us filling us with God's love, we will manifest His love in our lives through good and loving works toward others!

I would like to close this chapter with some scriptures to read and meditate concerning living this life of love. As we renew our minds to the Word of God, we will find it easier and easier to walk as Jesus walked upon the earth *(See 1John 4:17)*. We will go about doing good and destroying the works of the devil even as He did! *(See Acts 10:38)*.

And now abide faith, hope, love, these three: but **the greatest of these is love. Eagerly pursue and seek to acquire [this] love [make it your aim, your great quest]**...

1Corinthians 13:13 & 14:1(AMP)

I therefore, the prisoner for the Lord, appeal to and beg you to walk (lead a life) worthy of the [divine] calling to which you have been called [with behavior that is a credit to the summons to God's service. Live as becomes you] with complete lowliness of mind (humility) and meekness (unselfishness, gentleness, mildness), with patience, bearing with one another and making allowances because you love one another. Be eager and strive earnestly to guard and keep the harmony and oneness of [and produced by] the Spirit in the binding power of peace.

Ephesians 4:1-3(AMP)

Therefore be imitators of God [copy Him and follow His example], as well-beloved children [imitate their father]. And walk in love, [esteeming and delighting in one another] as Christ loved us and gave Himself up for us, a slain offering and sacrifice to God [for you, so that it became] a sweet fragrance...

Ephesians 5:1-2(AMP)

Fill up and complete my joy by living in harmony and being of the same mind and one in purpose, having the same love, being in full accord and of one harmonious mind and intention.

Philippians 2:2(AMP)

And this I pray: that your love may abound yet more and more and extend to its fullest development in knowledge and all keen insight [that your love may display itself in greater depth of acquaintance and more comprehensive discernment]. *Philippians 1:9(AMP)*

Also he (Epaphras) has informed us of your love in the [Holy] Spirit. *Colossians 1:8(AMP)*

Clothe yourselves therefore, as God's own chosen ones (His own picked representatives), [who are] purified and holy and well-beloved [by God Himself, by putting on behavior marked by] tenderhearted pity and mercy, kind feeling, a lowly opinion of yourselves, gentle ways, [and] patience [which is tireless and long-suffering, and has the power to endure whatever comes, with good temper]. Be gentle and forbearing with one another and, if one has a difference (a grievance, or complaint) against another, readily pardoning each other, even as the Lord has [freely] forgiven you, so must you also [forgive]. And above all these [put on] love and enfold your selves with the bond of perfectness [which binds everything together completely in ideal harmony]. *Colossians 3:12-14(AMP)*

But now that Timothy has just come back to us from [his visit to] you and has brought us the good news of [the steadfastness of] your faith and [the warmth of your] love…

1Thessalonians 3:6(AMP)

And may the Lord make you to increase and excel and overflow in love for one another and for all people, just as we also do for you. *1Thessalonians 3:12(AMP)*

May the Lord direct your hearts into [realizing and showing] the love of God and into the steadfastness and patience of Christ and in waiting for His return. *2Thessalonians 3:5(AMP)*

And we know (understand, recognize, are conscious of, by observation and by experience) **and believe** (adhere to and put faith in and rely on) **the love God cherishes for us. God is love**, and he who dwells and continues in love dwells and continues in God, and God dwells and continues in him. In this [union and communion with Him] love is brought to completion and attains perfection with us, that we may have confidence for the day of judgment [with assurance and boldness to face Him], because as He is, so are we in this world. There is no fear in love...

1John 4:16-18(AMP)

And now I beg you, lady, not as if I were issuing a new charge (injunction or command), but [simply recalling to your mind] the one (command) we have had from the beginning, that we love one another. *2John5(AMP)*

For you, brethren, were [indeed] called to freedom; **only [do not let your] freedom be an incentive to your flesh and an opportunity or excuse [for selfishness]**, but through love you should serve one another. For the whole Law [concerning human relationships] is complied with in one precept, You shall love your neighbor as [you do] yourself.

Galatians 5:13-14(AMP)

But the fruit of the [Holy] Spirit [the work which His presence within accomplishes] is love, joy, peace, patience (even temper, forbearance), kindness, goodness, faithfulness, gentleness (meekness, humility), self-control. Against such things there is no law [that can bring a charge]. *Galatians 6:22-23(AMP)*

Above all things have intense and unfailing love for one another, for love covers a multitude of sins [forgives and disregards the offenses of others]. *1Peter 4:8(AMP)*

Finally, all [of you] should be of one and the same mind (united in spirit), sympathizing [with one another], loving [each other] as brethren [of one household], compassionate and courteous (tenderhearted and humble). *1Peter 3:8(AMP)*

If you really keep the royal law in Scripture, "Love your neighbor as yourself," you are doing right. *James 2:8(AMP)*

Love (God's agape love) fulfills all the Law of God. In making God's immense, immeasurable love for us our Christian foundation and by being led by the Holy Spirit from within, we will be empowered and enabled to release His love out of our lives in joyful and creative expressions that will touch the lives of others with a little piece of pure Heaven on earth!

For brethren, ye have been called unto liberty; **only use not liberty for an occasion to the flesh**, but **by love serve one another**. For **all the Law is fulfilled in one word**, even in this; Thou shalt **love** thy neighbor as thyself. *Galatians 5:13-14 KJV*

Love does no wrong to one's neighbor—it never hurts anybody. Therefore **love meets all the requirements and is the fulfilling of the Law.** *Romans 13:10(AMP)*

Love never fails, and as we make God's love for us our solid Christian foundation, in Him we will never fail!